Rethinking Jewish Faith

SUNY Series in
Modern Jewish Literature and Culture

Sarah Blacher Cohen, Editor

Rethinking Jewish Faith

The Child of a Survivor Responds

STEVEN L. JACOBS

State University of New York Press

Published by
State University of New York Press, Albany

For information, address State University of New York Press,
State University Plaza, Albany, N.Y. 12246

Production by M. R. Mulholland
Marketing by Fran Keneston

Library of Congress Cataloging-in-Publication Data

Jacobs, Steven L., 1947-
    Rethinking Jewish faith : the child of a survivor responds /
Steven L. Jacobs.
        p.   cm. — (SUNY series in modern Jewish literature and
culture)
    Includes bibliographical references.
    ISBN 0-7914-1957-6. — ISBN 0-7914-1958-4 (pbk.)
    1. Judaism—20th century. 2. Holocaust (Jewish theology)
3. Holocaust, Jewish (1939-1945)—Influence. 4. Children of
Holocaust survivors—Religious life. I. Title. II. Series.
BM565.J35 1994
296.3'11—dc20   93-20865
                                                                        CIP
                                                                        Rev

10 9 8 7 6 5 4 3 2 1

For
Hannah Beth (born 29 November 1974),
Naomi Rachel (born 27 March 1977)
and
Shea (born 12 August 1985):

That the events of the past,
with which this book wrestles,
may ever remain so.

༄

*And for
Louanne:
My Wife, My Editor,
and
My Best Friend.*

A Meditative Reflection;
A Reflective Meditation

Contents

Foreword by Zev Garber   xiii

Foreword by Alan L. Berger   xvii

Introduction: Why? The Genesis of My Own Thinking   1

1. The Problem with God   13
2. Covenant: Involuntary? Voluntary? Nonexistent?   23
3. The Crises of Prayer   29
4. *Halakhah* and *Mitzvot*: Law and Commandments—
   The Heart of the Matter   37
5. Rethinking the Jewish Life Cycle: From Birth to Death   47
6. Rethinking the Jewish Festival Cycle:
   The Calendar in Question   63
7. Israel and Zionism in the Post-*Shoah* World   81
8. Rethinking Christianity: An Outsider's Perspective   89
9. Summarizing: Is Such Even Possible?   99

Appendixes   105

Appendix I: "[If] There Is No 'Commander'? . . .
   There Are No 'Commandments'!"   107

Appendix II: "Rethinking Jewish [and Christian?] Faith
   in Light of the Holocaust:
   The Response of the Child of a Survivor"   117

Notes and Bibliography   129

Glossary   141

About the Author   151

Foreword

A noticeable *Tendenz* among individuals who lived through the horrors of the German labor and death camps is to talk about their pre-World War II life and compare it to their experiences in Auschwitz, Buchenwald, Mauthausen, and other detention hell points. In addition, these tendency reports (oral and written) reveal the problems of Jews from decimated communities who try to go on with their lives after the war. Collectively, the eyewitness accounts talk of mental cruelty and physical torture, banishment and loneliness, and the inability of the survivors even to return to a state of normalcy. Still, a number of them devote themselves to examining through the *Shoah* experience in political action groups, outreach networks, and various forms of therapy.

The image-laden memories illustrate that the survivors of the *Shoah* are not saints but a group of ordinary people subjected to extraordinary stress and dehumanization, resulting for many in animallike acts of survivalism and regression to infantilism. However, Jews who endured suffering at the hands of Nazis were heroic on a much more basic human level, for certainly it is correct to view their endurance as being of heroic proportions. In word and in deed, these survivors were in control over the uncontrollable.

But how do we explain the inexplicable in terms of theology and religious obligation?

Noble Peace Prize laureate Elie Wiesel has observed on more than one occasion that the *Shoah* is the ultimate paradox: it imposes silence even while it imposes questions. At the closing convocation of the Oxford Conference on "Remembering the Future: The Impact of the Holocaust and Genocide on Jews and Christians" (July 10-17, 1988), he compared the *Shoah* to the revelation at Sinai: "Auschwitz seemed to me as anti-Sinai. Something essential was revealed there; it will take centuries to unravel its mysterious message."

In the most widely quoted passage in all of Wiesel's writings, we read of the shattering of innocence:

> Never shall I forget that night, the first night in camp, which has turned my life into one long night, seven times seven

cursed and seven times seven sealed. Never shall I forget that smoke. Never shall I forget the little faces of the children, whose bodies I saw turned into wreaths of smoke beneath a silent blue sky.

Never shall I forget those flames which consumed my faith forever.

Never shall I forget that nocturnal silence which deprived me, for all eternity, of the desire to live. Never shall I forget those moments which murdered my God and my soul and turned my dreams to dust. Never shall I forget those things, even if I am condemned to live as long as God Himself. Never.*

From Wiesel's writings we learn that there can be neither Auschwitz and no God, or God and no Auschwitz, but God and Auschwitz and Auschwitz and God. This Wieselian axiom is "the unbearable reality that haunts sleep and destroys wakefulness" (Robert McAfee Brown).

They who lived The Event and we who hear the cause and see the effect ask many imponderable questions, which unite in one: "What is a Jewish response to the anti-Sinai?"

Do we state that there is no God and Israel is His witness?

Do we declare with A. Roy Eckardt that "God is dead" or "Is He not dead?" are not the real concerns? The real question is whether, if God lives and is not helpless, ought He to go on living, He who has permitted the death of the innocent Six Million?

Do we follow Richard Rubenstein and let go of traditional Judaism's doctrine of God for a new symbol of God's reality conclusive to the lessons learned from Auschwitz?

Do we suggest Emil Fackenheim's 614th Commandment, meaning no posthumous victories for Hitler, and thereby acknowledge that "Rabbi" Hitler is the reason for Jewish being and existence?

Do we maintain Irving "Yitz" Greenberg's Voluntary Covenant and not Jewish tradition's Obligatory Covenant as a response to the shattered trust between God and Israel?**

Or is the response Elie Wiesel's witness-story, promoting Jewish survival as the unshakable dogma after Auschwitz?

---

*Elie Wiesel, *Night* (New York: Bantam Books, 1982), page 32.
**See Irving Greenberg, "Voluntary Covenant" in Steven L. Jacobs, ed., *Contemporary Jewish Religious Responses to the "Shoah"* (Lanham, Md.: University Press of America, 1993), pages 77-105.

Further, can meaningful Jewish commitment be passed on to the members of the "Second Generation," the children of survivors, whose family portrait has been abruptly shattered for all eternity? To say "Yes," and invoke God as theological proof positive is naive and misleading. God is not the all-perfect absolute of the philosophers nor the redeemer God taught in Jewish tradition.

Jewish tradition teaches that God did His job and gave Torah at Sinai so that the Jew and humankind can learn and do. But can many in the "Second Generation," who are not "true believers," read the Torah intact? Is one able to, does one care? Pogroms, expulsions, crematoria have blackened and scorged its words. Memory of its content is filled with family dead and broken divine promises. To seek the seer and scribe is to find ashes, shoes, and lamp shades.

In light of the *Shoah*, God appears not to rescue on the virtue of victim's distress nor do Jewish tears move the Lord of Mercy. God as a self-limiting *Borei Olam* (Creator God) willed an imperfect world so that humanity can be free and choose (or not choose) the right ethical action. "The *Shoah* demands," Steven L. Jacobs writes, "the reality that *humanity is free* to do to itself anything and everything of which it has always been capable, and only humanity, through whatever systems of checks and balances it alone is capable of devising, can save itself."

The author doubts that children of survivors can believe in an historically traditional God, however interpreted. In a previously published piece, he boldly proclaimed that there is no Commander and there are no commandments, and opined, "The reality of my world is that there is no longer any authority structure, other than that to which I would willingly subject myself, that has any authority over me."*

Thus, Jacobs is compelled to rethink Jewish deed and creed, and he painfully moves through Jewish covenantal categories (God, *mitzvot* and *halakhah*, holy passages, space and time), pausing whenever he wishes to illustrate a lesson, taking what appears to be a detour, until he returns to the true course. No doubt many readers will be disturbed by his forcible abandonment of the Torah-at-Sinai tradition in favor of a torah-from-cyanide stance, but others, impressed by the sight of the author's meditative reflection, will be perfectly confident that they have been all the while in good hands.

---

*Steven L. Jacobs, "[If] There Is No 'Commander'? . . . There Are No 'Commandments'!" *Judaism: A Quarterly Journal of Jewish Thought* 37, no. 3 (Summer 1988): 326.

A century ago, in 1892, the great cultural Zionist ideologue Ahad Ha'Am [1856-1927], wrote an essay, "Between Sacred and Profane," in which he explains the terms *sacred* and *profane* and how they are related to Jewish life. In his explanation, he uses an abstract philosophical concept, the distinction between "form" and "content." For Ahad Ha'Am, *content* is related to the purpose of an object or action, whereas *form* refers to the way in which the purpose is accomplished. In his own analogy, *form* is a wine barrel, and *content* is the wine it contains.

Ahad Ha'Am further observes that in profane matters the form exists for the sake of the content, but in sacred matters the form is every bit as important as what it contains, and if the content looses its significance, then the form is refilled with some new meaning. Similarly, for Steven L. Jacobs, the sacred forms of Judaism must continue for the "Second Generation" even though their contents have been tarnished forever. Knowingly or unknowingly, Jacobs fully understands Ahad Ha'Am's adage, the barrel that contains the wine is every bit as important as the wine itself, for should the barrel be broken, even the finest vintage would lose its taste.

As one travels with Jacobs in his journey, the reader discovers that this is not a work written in academic, dispassionate tone nor an attempt to "improve" post-*Shoah* Judaism by the use of abstract teachings. Rather, it is a personal rite of passage, a vindication of the author's right to observe those commandments and traditions that "give meaning to life" and contribute to a journey of inner healing. He asks questions and attempts answers but leaves many uncertainties unresolved. Yet uncertainty is truth in the making and the inevitable price of freedom.

Freedom of thought, honest reflection and the required commandment to study are the legacy of one man's *Shoah* reflection. It is a proper *teshuvah*—response and return—back from the twisted road to hell.

Zev Garber
Los Angeles Valley College
University of California at Riverside

Foreword

The existence of a second generation, daughters and sons of *Shoah* survivors, who self-consciously grapple with the meaning of their parents' experience is an important development in the study of the *Shoah* and its aftermath. Second generation membership is universal, reflecting the various countries where survivors built new lives. Brought to public attention in America during the late 1970s, the reflections of this group reveal much about the ferment of post-Auschwitz Jewish life and thought. Second generation members display a variety of orientations to Judaism ranging from Orthodox to atheist. However, all members of this group are defined and united by a central paradox: *The most important event in their lives occurred prior to their birth.* They are second generation witnesses, inheritors of a traumatic memory whose outlines were communicated both through verbal expression and by silence. Watching their parents' continuing survival, the second generation raised questions first about what had happened in the *Shoah* and then proceeded to inquire about the meaning of *the* defining event of the twentieth century. These questions are multiple, having artistic, psychological, sociological, and theological import. For example, "Where was God during the time of radical evil?" "Is it still possible, or important, to live a Jewish life?" "What is the meaning of a post-Auschwitz Jewish identity?" "Can Jews trust Christians? Or anyone?" Even as members of this generation are plagued by doubts that they are *entitled* to write about the *Shoah*, they cannot resist the obligation to do so.

The second generation has a particular angle of vision in their reflective process. Unlike their peers who are children of nonwitnesses, children of survivors know first hand the on-going impact of the destruction both on their parents' lives and on their own. They also understand the enormous significance of family and children. Moreover, they are committed to testify to the experience of the Jewish people during the *Shoah*. Consequently, this generation views the *Shoah* as both an historical event and a deeply personal trauma. With the passage of time, they have begun to bear their own witness to the destruction of Europe's Jews. Artistic, journalistic, psychological, and sociological reactions to the *Shoah* by this generation have already begun to appear. More will follow.

The reflections of Steven L. Jacobs form part of this mosaic of response. He speaks to the central theological issues of Jewish faith and identity after the *Shoah*. As the son of a survivor, his meditation is intensely personal, yet bears communal and interfaith significance. Entering the rabbinate was the author's answer to the destruction of family members who perished in the *Shoah*. But Jacobs goes further: Interrogating both God and humanity, history and tradition, he concludes that he is no longer able to affirm the traditional notion of God as the Lord of History. Consequently, in Jacobs's own words, "[If] There Is No 'Commander'? . . . There Are No 'Commandments!'" Yet, the author is committed to the necessity of meaningful Jewish existence. His meditation consists of an approach to achieving this task.

How can one remain Jewish after the *Shoah*? Jacobs argues that this question necessitates a re-visioning of all traditional teachings and concepts, beginning with God and the covenant. Jacobs also scrutinizes prayer and the meaning attributed to life-cycle events and festivals. For example, he suggests that God is a *Borei Olam*, Creator of the world, who in the process of creation withdraws from the world. The impenetrable barrier between such a God and humankind is part of the creative process and means that humans are totally responsible for the planet. Jacobs contends that, after Auschwitz, the Sinaitic covenant is no longer credible. He would substitute for it "covenants of dialogue" whose purpose is "to ensure global survival." Similarly, he calls for a reexamination of the rationale for all Jewish life-cycle events, dismissing all such rationales which understand God in an "historically traditional manner," as a deity who intervenes in history and responds to personal prayer.

Jacobs makes an intriguing suggestion concerning the "rethinking of Christianity." Rightly, he notes the need for a new Christian hermeneutic in reading the Scripture. From this should follow a reassessment of a Redeemer in an unredeemed world where Auschwitz occurred, the historic notion of Christian "mission" to the Jews, and a rethinking of the proper relationship between "parent" (Judaism) and "child" (Christianity). But Jacobs is hopeful on this score. He suggests that covenants of dialogue between Jews and Christians build bridges between the two groups and are important for two reasons. On the particular level, the need arises because of the fact that the *Shoah* happened. Universally, the threat of global destruction should unite people of good will.

This important study promises to elicit much response. Both its premise and conclusions are provocative in the sense of provoking one to think, and rethink, about theological issues after Auschwitz. The author's theological position will be debated both by his own peers and others. Likewise, his emphasis on study as the sole continuing post-Auschwitz commandment will find much resonance. His call for covenants of dialogue is one likely to be heard far and wide. Jews and Christians will have much to discuss and debate. In short, Steven L. Jacobs has written a study that, although it will anger some, perplex others, and give hope to yet a third group, cannot be ignored.

Alan L. Berger, Director
Jewish Studies Program
Syracuse University

Introduction: Why?
The Genesis of My Own Thinking

Introduction

The Jewish people—and all of contemporary humanity—is, at best, little more than a single generation away from the nightmarish events of the *Shoah* (Holocaust). Though the wound itself continues to fester—hardly a day goes by without the appearance of a new book, newspaper article, radio or television comment[1]—survivors and their offspring, as well as those only indirectly affected, continue to experience healing. Indeed, the very fact that there are offspring of those who experienced the unspeakable is, in and of itself, one measure of that healing. That this "Second Generation"—the offspring of the original survivors as we now are called and now choose to call ourselves—in turn chooses to have children furthers that healing, and may very well be the loudest response to Adolf Hitler's quest for a world *Judenrein* ("Jew free").

Problematic, however, is the literature that addresses the so-called inheritance of the Second Generation of victims—we children of diminished families—from the perspective of Jewish faith, belief, and practice. The concerns of too many writers are not with the *faith* of the Second Generation, and issues and concerns related to that faith, but rather with the psychological health and well-being of the children of survivors.[2]

Then, too, those Jewish writers who have directly confronted the *Shoah* and its religious and theological implications have profoundly and eloquently presented their thoughts to the worldwide Jewish community. But, like the "psychological school," they have not directly extended their thinking to the impact of the legacy of the *Shoah* upon the very generation who have now grown to maturity as adults, marriage partners, and parents, deeply affected by the experiences of their parents, still connected to and committed to the Jewish people and faith, but no longer either comfortable with or contented with the historically traditional responses of Judaism.[3] And further, to their own marriage partners and children who then become survivors

themselves (i.e., what we may very well call *inherited terror*[4]). Nor
have they practically and pragmatically addressed the concerns elaborated upon in this book.

That most Christian writers on the *Shoah* have not addressed
this particular audience comes as no surprise: The foci of their own
concerns have been two-fold: (1) building a bridge of reconciliation
with the Jewish people, and (2) making their own Christian communities more fully aware of the religious and philosophical, not to mention historical, implications of the *Shoah*.[5] To be sure, some of these
writers certainly have raised questions about religious faith in the aftermath of the *Shoah* that are relevant for the Second Generation as they
are for the First Generation. Moreover, the questions are equally per-
tinent for Christians, both those who lived through that period in
Europe or who escaped it by virtue of their distance or later birth.

Autobiography

What follows, then, is a *preliminary* investigation and exploration of those topic areas central to the Jewish religious experience by
one child of a survivor-escapee, now deceased, with a "look-see"
towards Christianity: (1) God, (2) covenant, (3) prayer, (4) *halakhah*
and *mitzvot*, (5) life cycle, (6) festival cycle, (7) Israel and Zionism,
and (8) Christianity. Before doing so, however, a bit of autobiography.

I was born in Baltimore, Maryland, on January 15, 1947, the son
of Ralph (nee Rolf) Albert Jacobs (born Rogowo, Poland, May 1, 1921;
grew up Zerbst, Saxony-Anhalt, Germany; died Gaithersburg,
Maryland, September 27, 1981) and Ruth Buchler Fyman (born New
York City, April 1, 1927). My father, a refugee from the carnage and
devastation of Hitler's Nazified Europe, escaped and came to this
country in December 1939, the only member of his immediate family
to do so. More than 150 members of our collective family were murdered at the hands of the Nazis and their henchmen; only 7 family
members, to the best of my knowledge, were spared: 5 to Baltimore,
Maryland, in 1933; 1 to Palestine in 1934; and one to Montevideo,
Uruguay, in the early 1930s. My mother's family, also German Jews,
had emigrated to this country in the late 1800s. My parents were married on January 19, 1946; I have one sister, three years younger, Elaine
Jacobs Waschler, who lives today with her daughter Lisa and son
Jeffrey in Scottsdale, Arizona.

Growing up in my parents' home in both Baltimore and Silver
Spring, Maryland, where we moved in 1958 and from where I left for
college and graduate school beginning in 1965, never to return for any

length of time, fills me with certain rather distinct memories of my father: Of his physically small stature (he was 5'6"; I am 6'2"), of his voracious appetite for reading (he read more than 100 books each year) primarily in the areas of World War II history, economics and political science (and retained what he had read!), of his intense dislike for his government job coupled with his need for economic security (he was a licensed journeyman printer), of his fervent Jewish and Zionist commitments and his renewable pain and difficulties with the *religious* aspects of his Judaism (brought up a German Orthodox Jew, his Orthodoxy "died in the camps"), of his nightmares and his loneliness.

Incidents too numerous to describe in detail obviously made a profound impact on me as I began to realize that the *Shoah* was, daily, part of our normative family experience. Being permitted to read any book in his library; hearing him tell and retell certain events about his parents and certain family members, all of whom were dead; associating his own loneliness with the absence of family at Thanksgiving, Chanukah, and other appropriate times—all this, it seemed to me, set us apart from other American Jewish families in the late 1950s and early 1960s. We were neither a particularly happy nor unhappy family, but we were *different* from others with whom I came into contact.

Our relationship, father to son and son to father, was not a particularly close one, grown softer, however, as I grew toward maturity and softened even more in the years since his death. His European background and child-rearing; his desire for me to "be a man," independent enough to survive as he himself survived, if such a tragedy should repeat itself; my own turbulent adolescence of anger and hostility toward that feeling of difference—all affected our relationship. Ultimately, however, his intellect, his quest for answers, and the *Shoah* itself led me on my own journey toward rabbinic ordination and Jewish scholarship.

My first career goal, for which and from which I graduated university, was as a high school teacher of English literature; love of education and learning was a dominating value in our home. But, increasingly, I grew dissatisfied with that choice, realizing early on that I simply could not relate to the specifics of the literary heritage I was teaching; it was not mine, no matter what I did to make it so. Judaism and Jewish learning, which I always enjoyed, *were* mine; and so I turned to that world in my own quest for meaning, authenticity, and self-validation.

Seminary training, however, although complete and full, was disappointing when juxtaposed to the *Shoah*. Courses in both philosophy and theology were, in truth, more survey than specific and never addressed specifically the philosophical and theological thinking and implications of those who concerned themselves with the *Shoah*. Courses in history likewise surveyed the richness of the Jewish past and present without examining in any depth whatsoever the *Shoah*. Elective courses, although far more specific in focus, were simply not offered in the *Shoah*—with one notable exception: During my second year [1970-1971], I had the opportunity to take the course and attend the additional lectures offered in the *Shoah* by the late (visiting) Professor Uriel Tal of Hebrew University, whose own pioneering research placed him at the very forefront of the landscape of *Shoah* historiography. Still the questions remained, looming ever larger.

Ordination, nonetheless, was for me a private and personal matter, not a public statement. It was my answer to the near-annihilation of our family; it was my "Yes!" that the family that I had never met, the ghosts who lived with me and within me, had not died in vain; that their murderous deaths were not meaningless. Though my original intention was to obtain my doctorate and teach in the newly emerging field of "*Shoah* Studies," I have primarily spent these last almost two decades in the service of the Jewish people, serving four congregations, one in Texas and three in Alabama, in addition to two so-called student pulpits in Ohio and New York. I have, in addition, been privileged to teach in three colleges and four universities, and have had more than fifty articles and book reviews and several books published covering the gamut of Judaic Studies, but focusing primarily on the *Shoah*. Still, however, the *Shoah* remains uppermost in my thoughts, unresolved.

The Questions

Questions of how and why are fundamentally intellectual, requiring, in this particular case, the processing of vast quantities of information in a variety of academic disciplines. For example, the history of antisemitism[6]—or anti-Judaism as some would prefer—dating far back into the pre-Christian Egyptian, Greek, and Roman periods is essential for a proper understanding of its evolution into the "biological antisemitism" practiced by the Nazis. Psychology of individuals; sociology of groups; philosophy and theology, Jewish and non-Jewish, as well as ancient, medieval, and modern history—all play significant and intertwined parts in attempts to come face to face with the realities of the abyss we call the *Shoah*.

Questions of *meaning* and *contemporary implications*, practical as well as theoretical, are far more difficult and are, only now, beginning to be asked on an increasingly frequent basis. Initially, what is required here is a certain distancing from the wounds, not necessarily healed, to ask those questions. First, as noted previously, what is asked in the realm of meaning is the theoretical, the speculative, the larger design, the "big picture." The philosophers and theologians who have addressed the *Shoah* thus far fall, in the main, into this category, Jewish or Christian. This book, then, is an attempt to address both the broader issues of God, covenant, and prayer, and the narrower issues of celebrating life cycle and calendar cycle in a disciplined historical religious tradition framed by *halakhah* (law) and *mitzvot* (commandments). It is, also, a blending of the two by addressing Israel and Jewish-Christian relations. In addition, the perspective from which these topics are approached is unique. Those who have thus far addressed them have done so from one of two vantage points: either they themselves have been the recipients of the horrors of the *Shoah*, or by and large, they have been contemporaneous with those events but thinkers about them nonetheless. As the mantle and burden of responsibility fall now to the inheriting Second Generation not to let the voices grow silent and the memories grow dim, it is up to us to reask many of the same difficult and troubling questions, accepting and rejecting previously supplied answers, and to add new ones, positing for ourselves and for other our own answers.

God

So I begin with God, the most troubling and problematic of all ideas and relationships when juxtaposed to the *Shoah*. Brought up with an enormous love and respect for the traditions of Judaism and the Jewish people, I was equally brought up with what I have taken to call the historically traditional notion and understanding of God: of a God who loves the Jewish people and who will save, protect, and care for them when dangers threaten and horrors unbidden present their ugly possibilities. Exposure to alternative ways of thinking about God in both undergraduate and graduate schools, although intriguing, made little significant impact upon me and, apparently, based on observation and experience, almost no impact whatsoever upon the Jewish people as a whole, whatever the denomination—Reform, Humanist, Conservative, Reconstructionist, Orthodox, Chassidic, Zionist, or Secularist. The God who could and did, according to Judaism's historically traditional presentation of itself and the vast majority of the Jewish people, did not, at least as far as the *Shoah* is concerned; and I am alone with my thoughts, attempting to crawl and climb out of the abyss into which I have now fallen.[7]

Covenant

From God to covenant, the central and enduring idea from which the Jewish people has bound itself to its God, sustained itself, and derived both strength and comfort in times of joy and sorrow. Covenant, *Brith*, the very symbol of the unique relationship between the Jewish people and God for better than 4,000 years, entered into at Sinai, according to Jewish tradition, and never abrogated. Now called into question because of the *Shoah*, the challenge remains: What kind of covenantal relationship makes sense with a God whose own actions or lack thereof during the years 1933[39]-1945 are extraordinarily difficult both to perceive and to understand? Has the *Shoah*, God forbid, nullified the covenant for ever and all time, rending it little more than an historic relic of Israel's past? Was there ever a time when the covenant protected Israel?

Prayer

And from God and covenant to prayer, the very vehicle by which the Jewish people, even before *Sefer Tehillim*, the Book of Psalms, have attempted to communicate with the Divine Presence. Israel's past and present is so very rich in the traditions of prayer; poetic, soulful words that speak across generations and give voice to the deepest longings and fertile yearnings of the human heart. What kinds of prayers now make sense? Petitionary? Thanksgiving? Adorative? Acknowledgment? Is prayer itself meaningful any longer? Is it worth the investiture and commitment of the religious?

Halakhah and *Mitzvot*

And on to *Halakhah* (law) and *Mitzvot* (commandments), the heart of the matter, and the unique way in which Judaism and the Jewish people have sought to engage in the Divine-human encounter and, equally, perpetuate the faith beyond its initial generation. Does this understanding of Divine Commander and law as the concretization of *His* commands any longer make sense in this post-*Shoah* world? Indeed, can there be any authority structure whatsoever—can there be any authorities whatsoever—other than those to which we willingly subscribe and willingly commit ourselves, always retaining for ourselves the right, responsibility, and freedom to say "No!"?

The Jewish Life-Cycle and Festival Cycle

The Jewish people and the individual Jew are defined by their on-going commitment to the twin calendars that govern Jewish life: the life-cycle calendar and the festival cycle calendar. Philosophy, theology, and history all provide windows of insight into these two calendars. The specific and uniquely Jewish ways in which this people chooses to mark the moments of the life's journey shared by all humanity, through its many and varied evolutions, coupled with events deemed of significance in the people's collective memory, set the Jewish people apart from its neighbors. The challenge, however, is not, nor has it ever been, with the specific changing practices of these two calendars. The challenge is with the *rationale*, the meaning behind the doing of both calendars. Given the years 1933[39]-1945, given the stark realities of the *Shoah*, given the murderous deaths of Six Million Jews, can Jewish events be celebrated and affirmed *for the very same reasons* they were celebrated and affirmed prior to 1933? Can these new historic realities be, somehow, incorporated into those celebrations without allowing them to dominate the events themselves? Is continuing to affirm the ages-old reasons for the doing of these events an ignoring of the *Shoah* itself and a desecrating assault upon the memories of the martyred millions?

The State of Israel

And what of the State of Israel, born out of the ashes of the *Shoah*, home now to more than 3 million Jews, home, too, for those survivors and their children who had nowhere else to go? What of Theodor Herzl's dream of a reborn Israel, safe and secure, a nation "like all the others," an answer to the antisemitism of Western Europe? Is the Zionist dream the only valid one or the ultimately valid one for the Second Generation and all other Jews in this post-*Shoah* world? Can Zion and Zionism be affirmed without *aliyah* (immigration)? Can Jewish life be affirmed wherever Jews now find themselves?

Christianity

And what of our neighbors, primarily Christians? What about our relationship to them and to that which they hold centrally precious and sacred? If Judaism needs to be rethought in light of the *Shoah*, does not Christianity, also, need to be rethought? Is it appropriate for a Jew to even suggest such a rethinking and reexamination of the fundamental precepts of the Christian faith without it being viewed as an attack by an outsider, which, in the long run, it may very well prove to be? Is the ultimate message of the rethinking of both Judaism and Christianity far broader in its implications than initially surmised, relevant now because of the *Shoah*, to all faith groups and faith communities? Does the *Shoah*, forever, end the supercessionist and triumphalist arrogance for far too long associated with the world's faiths? Is all such thinking heretical bordering on apostasy?

Problematic Answers

These are the questions asked and tentatively answered in this book by this Second Generation member, painful though they be. If our parents and grandparents, many no longer living, possess a credibility that enables them to speak out against the world's injustices because of what they themselves experienced, then we, too, share in that credibility as their legacy to us. If their voices are all-too-soon becoming silenced as the years since 1945 rush forward, then who, if not their children, will speak for them out of the crucible of our own experience and raise anew other, pain-filled questions, some, perhaps, for the very first time?

The question of why must also be asked? Why be concerned, if at all, with a rethinking and reformulation of the whole entire Jewish religious experience? Why not simply accept that which the various denominational factions within Judaism present as their understandings and reinterpretations of the Divine-human encounter? Or, if none is acceptable, why not reject them in their entirety, opting, instead, for secularism or secularist Zionism or, most radically, out of Judaism and the Jewish people altogether, as some have already done?

Because I am a Jew and choose to affirm both my Jewish self and my *religious* Judaism as the principal foci of my own Jewish identity in light of, or perhaps despite, the *Shoah*, the questions remain, ofttimes coming unbidden to consciousness, and, increasingly, demand answers. Because I choose to identify with *k'lal Yisrael*, the worldwide community of the Jewish people, others, too, I have found, raise the very same questions I am asking and discover themselves uncomfortable with answers already given and unable or unwilling to go elsewhere. Because my Judaism, my Jewish self, and my Jewish people remain centrally precious to me, and my commitment to *meaningful* and *creative* Jewish survival remains equally precious, what begins as a personal journey for me alone becomes, I hope, a contribution to that survival. Out of such wrestling and reflection comes growth.

The answers given will prove irksome to some and quarrelsome and troubling to others, and comforting, perhaps, to a small minority not usually addressed. Ideally, they will be discussed and debated by some, leading ultimately to further discussions and explorations of the issues raised, and finally to a new Jewish theological synthesis as we approach the twenty-first century. Realistically, however, they will be ignored by the majority of Jews and Jewish thinkers, who continue unwilling to confront head-on the theological and religious angst and implications raised by the *Shoah*. Other agenda continue to take precedence, and the religious voice of the Second Generation is seemingly lost among the din of other, always more pressing, concerns. But this voice is not yet ready to be silenced; it has only now begun to speak to a new generation possibly more willing to listen.

Positing new answers, in this particular case, in addition to the presumption of courage and the absence of immunity from serious and unrelenting criticism will require a further rereading of all of past and present Jewish history, theologically and philsophically. If the God of the *Shoah* is known by His absence, do we not need to rethink His very presence during the *Pesach* (Passover) liberation described in *Sefer Shemot* (Book of Exodus)—and all other subsequent examples of supposed Divine emancipation from evil? If the *Brith* (covenant) entered into at *Har Sinai* (Mount Sinai) ultimately proved of no avail, has it ever shown its viability? If the prayers of the righteous went unanswered during the *Shoah*, were there past occasions when they were, in fact, answered? And why not between 1939 and 1945? If the Jewish people formerly accepted the notion that life cycle, festival cycle, *Halakhah*, and *Mitzvot* all have their origins in Divine proscription and prescription, why not now? What has changed? Is it any longer possible to affirm the "political theology" of the Torah that *Eretz Yisrael* (*Land* of Israel), Zion, is a gift from God, His to do with as He pleases, mandating the dispersion and destruction of one people while inviting another to settle there? Does such religiously centered nationalism contain within itself the embryonic seeds of genocidal destruction of others or itself? What other, equally problematic questions present themselves vis-à-vis the Jewish experience when juxtaposed with the enormity of the *Shoah*? Cavalier dismissal of the questions and the questioner will not provoke either to go away; responding directly to the challenges presented can only further the cause of Judaism and the Jewish People.

Chofshi: Freedom

The answer to all of the preceding is, perhaps, contained within one Hebrew word, *chofshi*, "freedom." The constraints of the past by which the Jewish people has bound itself to itself, its traditions, and its God have been rendered asunder, perhaps for all time, by the realities of the *Shoah*. As will I believe become patently obvious throughout this book, the post-*Shoah* external imposition of authority makes little sense in our world; what does make sense is the desire, both on the part of the individual Jew and on the part of the Jewish people, both to be Jewish and to act Jewishly. That individual and collective will is, thus, the very real and evident source of renewed Jewish strength and commitment, enabling the American Jewish community to sustain its own vibrancy and the Israeli Jewish community to successfully defend itself against its enemies and keep open its doors to all who would enter. Never before in all of Jewish history have we Jews been presented with such a unique opportunity: to daily re-create Jewish life according to our own vision—without false or deceptive allegiance to a God in whom we do not believe or self-designated authorities to whom, in good and clear conscience, we could not affirm either fealty or loyalty.

Quite obviously, then, this book *is* a critique of old ways of thinking and doing Judaism, not out of any malicious intent to destroy what has been tortuously built over 4,000 years or designed to give succor to the enemies of the Jewish people. It is animated by the rabbinic dictum of *yesurin shel ahavah*, "chastisements out of love." Because I care, I take my critiques seriously out of my genuine desire to strengthen, always to strengthen. *Ayn breirah*, the *Shoah* permits me *no alternative* as a child of the Second Generation but to wrestle openly, honestly, and candidly with my Judaism, searching anew for answers where old ones no longer give comfort, attempting to forge yet a new synthesis as I make my way in the world.

That such wrestling in print may very well subject me to the criticism of *chutzpah*, brazenness, is accepted. That I would presume to know what is now the correct understanding and intepretation of the Jewish religious experience and tradition for the Jewish people in this post-*Shoah* world of the last decade of the twentieth century is a total misreading of what is contained herein. Rather, it is my small contribution to the on-going theological and religious debates within contemporary Judaism. (Errors of logic, thought or interpretation are, of course, totally my own.) Our strength here, too, is that we are not now nor have ever been a monolithic community of thought; our very vitality is derived from the clash of competing ideas, oft-times radically contradictory, synthesized anew in each and every generation. Only when we ignore the problematic, the uncomfortable, the distressing do we do ourselves, our Jewish people, and our Jewish tradition a disservice. History continues to present challenges to faith; the *Shoah* may very well be the most onerous of all challenges yet faced by Judaism and the Jewish people. But we will never know until we confront it directly, without blinders of any sort, open to all of its problems and its difficulties, weaving our way through the morass it has created for us.

Final Thoughts

That this book is dedicated to our children, Hannah, Naomi, and Shea, is as it should be; and with that fixed firmly in mind, this introductory essay comes full circle. The wrestling contained within the covers of this book is a journey of the mind, an intellectual, emotional, and spiritual struggle to come to grips with new, however painful realities, most assuredly frightening in their implications. These children, grandchildren of the survivors, the *Third Generation*, are the first for whom the *Shoah* is but a distant vision, a periodic reminder of a past perhaps left well enough alone as they themselves struggle anew to confront their own world and their own realities. They are, also, the first generation for whom the *Shoah* may very well recede into the dimmer recesses of consciousness, all but forgotten other than on suitable and proper occasions. Yet they, too, are inheritors of this same terrible legacy as their parents; and they, too, must be taught, along with their neighbors and friends, the awful and horrific details of this terrible tragedy if they are to participate in ensuring its nonrepetition. Historical knowledge together with philosophical and theological implications of the *Shoah* is, therefore, the place with which to begin. May this volume aid them in their journey, coming to whatever conclusions they themselves deem appropriate. And may the events of the past with which this book wrestles ever remain so.

Notes

1. The current Bosnian-Herzegovinian tragedy of "ethnic cleansing" on the part of the Serbs and Croats and their Muslim counterparts—and their obvious parallels to the Nazi policy of the Final Solution to the Jewish Problem—is but the latest example.

2. Here I am thinking primarily of the work of Martin Bergman and Milton Jucovy, Leo Eitinger and Robert Krell, Steven Luel and Paul Marcus, and even Helen Epstein, to a greater or lesser degree. (See "Notes and Bibliography" at the end of this book for full bibliographic citations.)

3. The writings of Eliezer Berkovitz, Arthur Cohen, Emil Fackenheim, Irving Greenberg, Bernard Maza, and of course, Richard Rubenstein come immediately to mind.

4. A term first coined by my wife Louanne.

5. The writings of Harry James Cargas, Alan Ecclestone, Alice Eckardt and Roy Eckardt, Franklin Littell, Michael McGarry, John Pawlikowski, David Rausch, Rosemary Radford Ruether, John Roth, Gerard Sloyan, among others, come equally to mind.

6. Defined concisely as "hatred of the Jewish People and/or Judaism" (i.e., the religious faith, heritage, and tradition of the Jewish people).

7. Among the distinguishing characteristics of the Jewish religious tradition, to be sure, is that of arguing with God, beginning with Abraham and his contesting the seeming Divine decision regarding the fate of Sodom and Gemorrah in *Bereshit* (Genesis). An excellent presentation of this tradition is the book by Anson Laytner, *Arguing with God: A Jewish Tradition* (Northvale, N.J.: Jason Aronson, 1990).

1

The Problem with God

Both the Torah and postbiblical or Pharisaic-Rabbinic Judaism (not to mention Christianity) present their own understandings of God as the "God who acts in history," whose caring concern for Jews (and Christians) was ultimately expressed at Sinai (and Calvary), for reasons largely unknown to His human children. No longer acceptable or comforting to this Jew, however, when juxtaposed to the *Shoah* is the midrashic, that is interpretive, understanding of a God who, sadly, went with His children into exile and slavery in Egypt and rejoiced, gladly, with them when they celebrated their liberation from that slavery and bondage, but was seemingly absent between the years 1933 and 1945, or more specifically, between 1939 and 1945. No amount of contemporary religious rationalization can overcome the enormity of the loss of Six Million Jews—more than 150 members of my own family. Little, if any, comfort, it seems to me, can be derived from the idea that Providence prevented that number from escalating higher. If truth now be told, for some among us today, not only were Six Million of our Jewish brothers and sisters murdered in the *Shoah*, as well as Five Million non-Jews, but the historically traditional notion of God also died in the concentration and death camps that now puncture the landscape of Europe. *What is now demanded in the realm of theological integrity is a notion of God compatible with the reality of radical evil at work and at play in our world, a notion that, also, admits of human freedom for good or evil—without the fruitless appeals to a God who "chose" (?) not to act because He could not act.* To continue to affirm the historically traditional notion of faith in God as presented by both Torahitic and Pharisaic-Rabbinic traditions (as well as Christianity) is to ignore the *Shoah* with all of its uniqueness and to ignore those who, like myself, continue to feel the pain of family loss, yet want to remain committed to Jewish survival—not because God wills it, but because without even this most fragile of moorings, we are cut off from our battered community.

Such a different and differing understanding of God is, however, contingent upon accepting the *Shoah* as a radical extension of preceding Jewish history and experience, although a number of earlier destructions in Jewish history many now be seen as indicative of a need to change the understanding of God even at those times (as a few individuals seem to have considered). Not that it *should* have happened, but that it could and did happen, given the centuries of antisemitism and the pre-prepared environment that preceded it. Debates may still rage within both Jewish and Christian scholarly and religious circles as to the necessary, sufficient, or proximate causes of the *Shoah*, but for this child of a survivor-escapee and children of other survivors, armed with even a minimal knowledge of Jewish history and tragedy, the *Shoah* is literally "something else" and must be so regarded or ignored. How else, then, to understand the shift from pre-Christian cultural and social antisemitism to and through Christian religious and theological antisemitism to and through the Enlightenment and post-Enlightenment political antisemitism to the "biological" antisemitism of the Nazis from which no Jew could escape, including the members of one's own family? How else to understand the very modernity of the *Shoah* as the historically-validated marriage of bureaucratic excellence and technological perfection that perceived *Die Endlosung*, the "final solution" (to the Jewish problem), within the realm of human possibility? How else to confront the pain of loss, daily self-evident, and even haltingly, begin to make some sense of it?

Such an understanding is, likewise, contingent upon accepting a notion of God as other than historically and traditionally presented and understood by both Judaism and Christianity. One possible source of Divine affirmation, to the degree to which such affirmation is either desired or acknowledged as desired, lies in the concept of a "limited God" who could neither choose nor reject action during the dark years of 1933(39)-1945, who could not have responded to those humanly created and crafted processes of destruction even if He or She had wanted to do so. Notions of omniscience, omnipotence, omnibenevolence, and the like quickly fall by the wayside. The alternative possibilities, it seems to me, are a God who was ignorant of the designs of His or Her German children and their European cousins, and impotent to act even after learning of their plans. Or a *limited God* whose own nonknowledge and limited power precluded both foreknowledge and interference. The very *technology* of Nazism has forever shattered the easy appeal to a God who will, somehow, curb the limits of human intellect and action for evil or good and, in the future, prevent a repetition or recurrence of the *Shoah* or *Shoah*-like genocides. If anything, the reverse is now possible: Having let the genie of destructive technology out of the bottle of human ignorance, our best hope of containment for Jewish and human survival lies not in the heavens above but in our ability to educate the next generation to evince the same intellectual expertise and curiosity to creative measures as have thus far been evinced to destructive measures.

Where, then, do we begin to construct such a theological understanding of God that addresses these realities? Where, then, do we now begin to find such a God?

I would propose we begin with a Creator God, but, equally, with an understanding of that creative process significantly different than previously presented—at variance, to be sure, with the Torahitic and postbiblical Pharisaic-Rabbinic (and Christian) presentations of God. So be it, then.

All human experience tends to confirm the idea of the creator-creation relationship, whether that relationship is sustained, on-going, or severed after the initial point of contact. Simply put, *it makes more sense to believe in a Creator God who initiated a process of creation by which the world as we know it—not as we would wish it—came to be*; our own desire, as children to parent, as subjects to ruler, as students to teacher, as congregants to rabbi, is for that relationship to be on-going and sustained, whether or not such is actually the case. For the scientifically minded, the question is not whether the so-called gaseous hypothesis or big bang theory more adequately describes the creation of the world or universe—or any other postulated theory for that matter. That there exists (or existed) an *Initiator* worthy of our respect, admiration, acknowledgment, adoration, praise, appreciation, thanksgiving, or what have you is the proper purview of the religionist or the theologian—whether or not that Initiator continues to manifest interest in His or Her creation, whether or not that Initiator can communicate with Its creation, whether or not that creation can communicate with its Initiator. (The specific context of such communications is the subject of Chapter 3, "The Crisis of Prayer.")

The "logic model" of creation, which makes the most sense to me, which I would therefore present, and which seems to address the *Shoah* specifically and all human and Jewish tragedy generally is the following: For reasons always and forever unknown to humanity, the initiating, creator God chose to initiate a creative process by which the world or universe as we know it, and as we presently understand it, came to be. Prior to that moment, or series of moments I know not which, only God Himself or Herself existed. The phrase that best describes that act of creation for me, therefore, is that God "withdrew into Himself or Herself," leaving a formless, chaotic void (echo of biblical tradition) wherein that creation—world, universe—would, ultimately, come to be. In so doing, however, as born out by the experience of human history, not only Jewish, in the very act of creation, an *impenetrable* barrier arose, one that could not be transcended in action, word or thought by either God or humanity, both of whom are, in fact, limited. Whether or not the erection of this barrier was by accident, or as a by-product to this initially creative act, or by design, so committed was (and is?) God to allowing this creation the fullest possible freedom in the exploration of its own potential, I know not which. Besides, it ultimately remains a moot question; what is at issue is not the reason behind this barrier, but that this barrier exists and cannot now or ever be transcended by either God or humanity as borne out by the realities of history.

Thus, one shifts one's focus in a variety of directions all at the same time: The issue is no longer God's interest, lack of interest, indifference, or hostility toward the humanity community. *Since the initial act of creation, God can no longer interact with His or Her creation, transcend the barrier if you will, even if He or She would wish to do so.* Nor can humanity equally transcend this same barrier asking, pleading, begging for Divine intervention. *Human tragedy, therefore, the Shoah included, is fully, totally, and completely the result of human action or inaction.* After creation, we human beings are, ultimately and absolutely, responsible for the past, present, and future of this planet and for the populations that reside on it. Historically naive appeals to Deity for succor spring from the non-recognition that such a barrier truly exists. Evidence of supposed Divine interaction results from perceiving the realities of historical situations through prefocused theocentric lenses. "I saw the hand of God saving me because I knew I would see the hand of God saving me."

The alternative view to this, for this child of a survivor-escapee, confronts the very arbitrariness of the Deity and raises far more questions than it even remotely attempts to answer. If God did, in fact, rescue the Jewish people from the hell of Egyptian slavery, why not rescue us from the hell of Auschwitz or Buchenwald or Maidanek or Mauthausen?[1] If God did, in fact, redeem the Jewish people from our exile in Babylonia, why not redeem us after our exile in Riga or Kovno or Lidice or Lvov? If God saved us after our departure from Spain only 450 years before, why not save us after our departure from the cities, towns, villages, and countries throughout Eastern and Western Europe, where we have lived for over 1,000 years and from where we were taken to ghettos and on to concentration camps and murderous death?

Could it be that God did not rescue, redeem, save us during the *Shoah* because God *chose* not to do so for reasons either unfathomable or too monstrous to contemplate? Could it be that we, somehow, *merited* such punishment as the result of our own errant way or the ways of the rest of humanity, serving, once again, as their *korban*, their sacrifical offering? What possible sin or sins had we or they committed that necessitated the deaths of so many innocents along with the guilty, especially children, Jews and non-Jews alike, in ways so horrific as to border on the unspeakable and unbelievable?

Or could it be that God did not rescue, redeem, save us during the *Shoah* because God *could not* do so, however much God wanted to do so? Again, the impenetrable barrier. Much as I would want to believe God *wanted* to redeem our Jewish people during the *Shoah*, the full weight of the evidence indicates that God did not do so. And such desire without resolute action, to my way of thinking, equates with impotence. Better, perhaps, to maintain the illusory notion that God wanted to do so but was unable to do so rather than accept the notion of a God who could not or would not do so. But, if anything, the thoughts contained within this book are, equally, an attempt to confront those very illusions that have, heretofore, provided—again to my way of thinking—a false sense of both hope and security oft-times with tragic results. As the child of a survivor-escapee, then, religious illusions, too, are casualties of the *Shoah*.

To be sure, the position just suggested parallels that of the European, and American to a lesser degree, philosophical and religious existentialists who gained currency during the 1960s and early 1970s. For them, the universe as we know it and experience it is one of random accident and chance, God playing no part whatsoever in its on-going day-to-day processes, despite however much we would like it to be otherwise. The oft-echoed response to human tragedy "Why me?" or "Why us?" becomes, instead, "Why not you?" either singularly or in the plural. In such a universe, it is not that such and such a specific tragedy *must* happen, but that, given everything that constitutes humanity, such and such a tragedy *can* happen and, given past human history, has, more often than not, happened. Our naturally human desire of wanting to be spared such tragedy for ourselves and our families, although understandable, is, therefore, inconsistent and illogical. Sadly, human tragedy is, thus, the result of the very arbitrariness of our universe, not the arbitrariness of God, the "luck of the draw"; God now becoming irrelevant in the process.[2]

Recognition of the validity of this understanding does nothing to diminish either the religious nature of humanity or humanity's response to the universe. But it, too, like the aforementioned understanding of creation, goes a long, long way toward moving beyond the false and illusory hope of attempting to reconcile a loving, interactive God with the tragedy of the *Shoah*. It, also, removes forever from all human understanding the naive and infantile idea of an interactive God protective of His or Her human children.

Almost immediately, however, the secondary question arises: "Could, therefore, such a tragedy as the *Shoah* have been prevented, given this understanding of its entirely human character?" In theory, it could have been averted; in practice, given the sad state of our knowledge of human behavior under the most adverse and extreme of conditions, it is highly unlikely. Having not learned the lessons of previous examples of genocidal behavior, there is little in human experience, to this point, to suggest that, prior to Adolf Hitler's ascension to the chancellorship of Germany in 1933, following his published vision of the future in *Mein Kampf* in the mid-1920s, the *Shoah* could have been averted. All of which is to say absolutely *nothing* about God. Could humanity have spared itself repeated excesses of genocidal behavior? Perhaps. Could God have, somehow, intervened to spare us these tragedies, in particular the *Shoah*? Not at all.

At this point, with what then are we left in our halting attempt to understand God and God's relationship to planet earth and its inhabitants? With a limited God initiating a process of creation, but, in all candor, unable to move beyond a barrier imposed by that very act of creation. Although more fully explored in Chapter 3, our *initial* response, therefore, must be one of recognition, acknowledgment, and thanksgiving, even while recognizing that any such verbal response moves not at all beyond human hearing: "Thank you God for initiating a process whereby I came to be" may prove, definitively, the only legitimate form of prayer, directed inward rather than outward, enabling me to perceive myself far more humbly than history has thus far indicated has been humanity's perception of itself. It may, also, enable me to realize the essential equality that inherently exists among all creation, not only human, and to begin to think and develop strategies that emphasize this equality rather than the ego- and power-oriented systems of both past and present if our planet is to survive.

Thus, when this understanding of creator God is juxtaposed with the *Shoah*, a lesson to be learned presents itself, starkly and dramatically: *Humanity cannot, now or ever, depend on God to and for its very survival, but must depend upon itself and its very willingness to develop interdependent links as the only reasonable opportunities and possibilities for that survival.*

What of our *need* for God? Does not what has thus far been written entirely negate that need? To be sure, what is now negated is an understanding of God inconsistent with the realities of history, especially the tragic history of the *Shoah*. My *need* for God is that need to recognize this fundamental truth of the universe and, somehow, to release from deep inside of me that caring and compassion which will ensure that genocide, even as it is now being practiced, will not continue ever again to haunt humanity. Having been the inheritor of the *Shoah*, I cannot allow myself the luxury of silence in words or actions in the face of genocide. What was for my family could very well be again for my family if those who would orchestrate such scenarios are permitted free reign against others in the human community, if their murderous schemes and designs are allowed to go unchecked.

Thus, we must accept, because the *Shoah* demands that we accept, the reality that *humanity is free* to do to itself anything and everything of which it has always been capable; and only humanity, through whatever systems of checks and balances it alone is capable of devising, can save itself. The oft-quoted rabbinic dictum "Everything is foreseen, but free will is given" made sense only in a world where the rabbis' understanding of God was that of the historically traditional ideas and ideals expressed early on in this chapter and in the Introduction. Having presented anew the understanding of a limited, creator God, everything is no longer, nor has it ever been, foreseen or preordained! Free will, the ability of humanity to continue to explore all aspects and facets of its potential, for evil *and* good, is, evidently, the result of the creative process itself, which, once initiated, remains unchecked unless we ourselves decide to check it. Subject to our own passions, ruled always by both head and heart, we are, ultimately, constrained only by our finitude and the finitude of others, but not by appeals to a supposed "Higher Power."

Evil, too, is equally part of this same creative process initiated by God. It is, however, solely and totally the result of our own doing and devising. It is not that we humans are inherently evil; it is that we are, like the very process of creation itself, creatures of potential for good and evil, unfettered by Divine chains. Human evil, therefore, must be equated not with death or natural disaster, the former always a certainty and the latter always a possibility, but with those actions that result in the destruction of persons or groups without either their consent or their desire to participate in their own demise. Such destruction of others that causes pleasure or pain to its initiators *is* evil and must be so regarded as such. Such human evil cannot be stopped either by appeals to God or by intervention of that same God, but only by humanity's own willingness, through education and moral and legal safeguards, both to stop it once started and prevent it from ever having been started.[3]

Equally, too, blaming this limited God for human evil or for the potential for evil that resides in all humanity is both pointless and fruitless. Having already recognized God's inability to intervene or interact in human affairs, how can we fault God for what we do to ourselves? To be sure, some among us would fault God for having "endowed" us with the capacity for evil. But that, too, is a misreading of the creative process initiated by this limited God who was not fully knowledgable about the so-called end result of creation when it came to us human beings. Human potential is synonymous with human energy, and when coupled with, but not necessarily ruled by, either mind or heart, destruction is as likely a result as is any other possibility.

Limiting God as the *only* religiously rational answer to the horrors of the *Shoah* likewise gives rise to the whole question of Divine eternality, but this question, too, becomes moot. An eternal God no longer involved with or capable of involvement with this creation is of little concern to humanity. A limited God of limited life's duration, even one shortened by or after the initial act of creation, although an intellectual possibility, does nothing to change the reality of what continues to transpire on this planet. Like the aforementioned existentialism of the early 1960s and 1970s, the "God is dead" movement somewhat popular on college campuses during this same period was more an exercise of words and language rather than a confrontation with either creation or evil historically or contemporarily considered. Affirming the limited nature of God precludes any meaningful discussion of God's eternality from the vantage point of understanding the *Shoah*.

Let us, therefore, leave this limited God, no longer, if ever, responsible for the *Shoah*, whose responsibilities to humanity ended with the initial act of creation, and address the singularly unique historically traditional understanding of the relationship between God and the Jewish People, that of the *Brith* or covenant.

Notes

1. To regard the former as a *singular event* incapable of repetition still remains problematic: Why one and not the other? Did God, somehow, therefore, expend whatever energy committed to human interaction on the *Pesach* liberation and have none left during the *Shoah* even though Jews and Christians regard *all* prior rescues as Divine interventions?

2. Such an explanation is equally applicable to a "theology of natural disaster," whereby such devastating events as earthquakes, hurricanes, tornados, and the like are no longer seen as the result of the "active hand of God," but rather possibilities within the world of the possible.

3. The work of such thinkers as Israel Charny, Jerusalem, and Franklin Littell, Philadelphia, about the need for a "genocide early warning system" is hereby acknowledged and appreciated. Much, much more work, however, needs to be done in this area, foremost among which is the fullest exploration of the international legal ramifications of such a system and its impact upon individual nation-states.

2

Covenant: Involuntary? Voluntary? Nonexistent?

The notion of *Brith* or "covenant" that has remained as the very essence of Israel's faith and relationship between itself and its God must now be re-thought and redefined in light of the *Shoah*. A violated but never abrogated Torahitic understanding of covenant makes sense only in relationship to that God who acts in history. Why bother with any other? Covenant with God, whereby both God and Israel agree to certain stipulations in order to maintain harmony and equilibrium is no longer logical nor desirable outside of such historically traditional ways of thinking, nor has it ever been. Irving "Yitz" Greenberg's "voluntary covenant" becomes an option only for those who wish to enter into it—as does its opposite, a rejection of the entire enterprise.[1] The *Shoah* forces us to confront reality on a starkly tragic plane whether we wish to do so or not. Therefore, we can no longer trust in our supposed covenantal relationship with God to keep the enemy from crouching at our door, to use the biblical-prophetic metaphor. Nor can God, however we choose to understand Him or Her, trust us not to act in ways that would prove either a one-time or perpetual violation of sacred trusts as regards the living things of our earthly home. If we are now to enter into religiously sensitive and renewable covenants, they must be with each other as individuals, as communities, as nation-states. Humanity having now actualized and demonstrated the potential to destroy larger and larger groups, we Jews having now been the recipients of such destruction, together, we must guard against repetition by our continual willingness to engage in dialogue, despite our differences, even with those whose value systems we fundamentally reject. Historically and contemporarily, Russians and Americans, Jewish and Christians, Jews and Jews, Jews and Arabs, Jews and Palestinians, Jews and Germans,[2] Christians and Christians, Christians and Arabs, must, in fact, enter

into "covenants of dialogue" to ensure the survival of all people on
our planet. We *must* commit ourselves to searching out those who
can best bring about such covenants of dialogue between seemingly
disparate groups. Appeals to God will not make such dialogues possible, nor will appeals to historical relationships or nonrelationships.
Only direct appeals to each other will. Our very survival depends on
it. Notions of politics or "one-ups-person-ship" have no place whatsoever in such calls to "covenants of dialogue."

Such dialogues, therefore and initially, require any number of difficult commitments, foremost among which is a radical rethinking of
the whole notion of the "other." True, honest, and open dialogue
among opposites now demands an intellectual, emotional, and spiritual integrity and respect more so than ever before. Group representatives must now meet as true equals with no so-called hidden agendas
whatsoever. The purpose of all such "covenants of dialogue" is the
mutual sharing of information and the setting forth of common agendas and agreements. Respect for differences in attitudes, perspectives, and orientations to problem solving must be affirmed no matter
how difficult they at first appear.[3]

Let us return, however, to the supposed covenantal relationship that seemingly existed between the God of Israel and the people
of Israel, now rendered asunder by the very force of the *Shoah*. Can it
any longer be affirmed in any manner, way, shape, or form? *The
answer is, sadly and tragically, "No!"* The ideas of both an "involuntary" covenant as it has presented itself throughout all past Jewish
history, according to the *Sefer Devarim (Book of Deuteronomy)*
entered into at Sinai by those physically present, as well as the generations still to come, and Greenberg's permutation of it as a "voluntary" covenant in light of the *Shoah* no longer prove tenable in the
world in which we now find ourselves. As already stated in Chapter 1,
God could not and did not protect us from the horrors of the *Shoah*;
therefore, to continue to affirm that historically traditional understanding of covenant flies in the face of Jewish and all human experience.

Additionally, and, again, because the concept of *Brith* as it originally developed in the Torah makes sense only in relationship to that
historically traditional understanding of the God who acts in history,
the sad and tragic lesson of the *Shoah* is that this concept, too, is, in
truth, a casualty of the *Shoah*. Thus, the relationship between God
and the Jewish people must now be redefined, if at all possible, to
somehow encompass a concept of God no longer dependent upon
the *Brith* as well as a concept of the *Brith* no longer dependent upon

God. The evidence has now been presented: *The Jewish people can no longer imagine, assume, or presume to call upon God because of our preexisting relationship as reflected in the Brith to protect us from the horrors of what we human beings can do and have done to ourselves. God's ultimate failure to save or protect the Jewish people during the Shoah invalidates any belief in the efficacy of the Brith itself and any claim the Jewish people might otherwise have to call upon God for active involvement, including, but not limited to, intervention or rescue.* By extension, redefinition raises the honest possibility of no continuing, on-going relationship between God and the Jewish people at all and, in its wake, calls upon us to reread all past Jewish historical experiences as we determine whether or not our predecessors accurately read or misread their own events covenantally.

Corollary to this notion of the *Brith* is that of the "election of Israel," as the so-called Chosen People of God. Can this idea, too, be affirmed in any *positive* sense in light of the *Shoah*, realizing now only too well that Hitler, Himmler, and their Nazi minions did, indeed, "choose" the Jewish people for annihilation, extermination, and obliteration from the face of the earth?

Historically and traditionally understood, the Torahitic concept of the Chosen People, much maligned and regularly misperceived by Western civilization, asserts that collective Israel was *chosen* by God to be a witness to His Divine reality and to the way of life He chose to share with Israel at Sinai. For reasons largely unfathomable, this numerically, economically, politically, and militarily insignificant nation was to be the recipient of a wonderous gift far beyond its relatively minor status in the world. Internally misconstrued by the Jewish people itself, the concept of the Chosen People had led, at times, to a misplaced sense of the superiority of self and the inferiority of others, bordering, perhaps, on arrogance. Externally misconstrued, it has led to jealousy, envy, a desire to usurp the position of Israel as "God's elect" and repeated attempts to remove Israel from the world scene through (1) ghettoization, (2) expulsion, (3) forced conversion, or (4) extermination, or some combination of any or all of them.[4]

Now, almost five decades after the closure of World War II, does the Jewish idea of the Chosen People make sense positively? *The answer is, sadly and tragically, "No!"* What other conclusion can we Jews come to in light of the *Shoah* except that, early on, we misunderstood our relationship with God and suffered the consequences because of it and because the non-Jewish world equally chose, for its own self-serving reasons, to continue this "myth of misunder-standing."

A far more accurate understanding of Israel's relationship to God is not that of a Chosen People but that of a Choosing People: a people who glimpsed correctly a reality far unlike anything the world had heretofore experienced and, over the centuries, continues to affirm the truth of that reality by its willingness to pay whatever price is exacted of it. *We are God's witnesses that God exists, or at least existed, however we now choose to understand that God, however our neighbors, for good or ill, now choose to understand that God.*

Furthermore, having now rejected both the concepts of the *Brith*, covenant, and the Chosen People, we are now confronted with something of a terminological problem: What word or words can we now best use in light of the *Shoah* to describe our post-Auschwitz understanding of God, God's relationship or nonrelationship with the Jewish people throughout all past Jewish history? Having con-cluded that both *Behirah*, "chosenness," and *Brith*, "covenant," are no longer viable—if, indeed, they ever were—what descriptors now present themselves? Having concluded in Chapter 1 that the "God of the Jews" is no longer a vital partner actively involved in pursuing, strengthening, expanding, protecting any relationship whatsoever with the Jewish people, what word or words is now best, then, to describe the current state of affairs?

Honesty demands, the *Shoah* itself demands, words, concepts, ideas, and ideals religiously and theologically compatible with this latest historical experience of the Jewish people. To do and say oth-erwise is delusionary, both individually and collectively. Thus, we are now forced to admit that the "covenant concept," so long a source a strength and inspiration for generations of Jews is now *nonexis-tent*, whether or not it has ever been existent. Thus, we are now compelled to confess that the concept of "chosenness," equally a source of strength and inspiration, no longer provides the psycho-logical comfort and armor it did prior to 1933. The uniqueness of collective Israel's perspective on the Divine-human and human-human encounters must be, forever and all time, now expressed in human terms. If, indeed, "the truth shall set you free," then we Jewish people are now free to chart our present and future destinies, no longer bound to concepts that our historical experience of 1933(39)-1945 shattered into fragments impossible to resurrect ever again. *We will do what we will do, we will say what we will say, we will think what we will think, and we will believe what we will believe, no longer tied to past ways of doing, saying, thinking, and believing.*

Our freedom to survive in this post-*Shoah* world as a particularlistic community, always willing to learn from our past but no longer afraid to move beyond it in thought and action, now depends upon our examination of the *Shoah* with all of its implications with eyes, hearts, minds, and souls open wide. For us Jews at the end of the twentieth century, it is the one phenomenon we cannot ignore if we are to fully prepare ourselves to meet and greet the twenty-first century.

Having now addressed both God and covenant-chosenness, we now turn to the concept of prayer, the way in which we humans, especially we Jews, have long sought to communicate with the God whom we always believed communicated with us.

Notes

1. See Irving Greenberg, "Voluntary Covenant," in Steven L. Jacobs, *Contemporary Jewish Religious Responses to the Shoah* (Lanham, Md.: University Press of America, 1993), pages 77-105.

2. Following the *fact* that, during the darkest days of the *Shoah*, representatives of the organized worldwide Jewish community met with Nazi representatives in an ultimately fruitless effort to save Jewish life, but they met nonetheless.

3. I have long envisioned, for example, the creation of an Institute for Interreligious Understanding and Dialogue, associated with a college or university, that, through conferences and scholarly publications, would explore the difficulties and inherent tensions in all such dialogues.

4. Raul Hilberg's magisterial three-volume *The Destruction of the Jews*, revised and definitive edition (New York: Holmes and Meier, 1985) summarizes this pattern succinctly as the movement from "You have no right live among us as Jews" to "You have no right to live among us" to "You have no right to live."

3

The Crises of Prayer

Prayer, too, like so much else, now stands in need of rethinking in light of *Shoah*. Appeals to God to correct present situations or to dramatically alter future possibilities have now proven themselves of no avail. To now expect God to respond on a less frightful level to less critical pleas is, to my way of thinking, theological absurdity, having realized no response from On High to words spoken in earnestness and fervor during the long dark night of Nazism's all-too-successful reign of terror. Unless, of course, we are prepared to accept a God able to deal with only the inconsequential rather than the consequential, equally a theological absurdity. Prayer will now have to become an internal plea, given voice and thought, for recognition that

1. the universe does manifest certain harmonies if we are but receptive to them;
2. creation allows us more possibilities for human growth than does destruction;
3. aesthetic appreciation of our world enhances our pleasure at being part of it;
4. the prayerfully poetic words of our predecessors, both Jewish and Christian, contained with the *siddurim* (sabbath and festival prayer books) and *machzorim* (High Holy Day prayer books) of both religious traditions, now reinterpreted since the *Shoah*, likewise increase the shared yearnings of all humankind for peace and survival;
5. the disciplined gatherings of like-minded groups in celebration and in sorrow can help energize us to confront the challenges of our own day and learn from each other;
6. last and perhaps most important, we need not suspend our intellect nor deny historical realities, especially those of the *Shoah*, when we engage in what we will continue to call *prayer*.

We will take each in turn.

Creative scientific thinkers at the cutting edge of their own disciplines, such as James Gleick, John Briggs, and F. David Peat, among
others, are want to speak of "chaos theory" in relation to the universe. For the rest of us, our "comfort level" of human existence is sustained by the "simple" (not simplistic!) knowledge that

1. this planet is not directly headed towards either the sun or the
    moon, nor are other planetary bodies headed directly toward us;
2. planet earth is not immediately in danger of extinction as the
    result of *external* forces;
3. the rhythm of all life's existence is that of birth, growth, matura-
    tion, decay, and death, by plant, animal, and human;
4. the things we create are far from infinite, most will "wear out,"
    planned or unplanned, prior to our own demise, though some
    will outlast us;
5. ideas, ideals, beliefs, and relationships are, ultimately, what sus-
    tain us and best enable us to move positively from one plane of
    our existence to the next.[1]

Acknowledgment of these verities and acceptance of their unal-
terable and, to my way of thinking, eternal realities should produce in
us a true sense of both our place and our role in the "grand scheme of
things" in this universe. Be we arrogant or humble, presumptuous
or modest, stiff-necked or flexible, powerful or powerless, ego centered or other centered, self-serving or self-effacing, the life's journey common to all humanity is the same. Endowed with the possibility to shorten both our own journey as well as that of others,
continually tantalized by the scientific possibility of lengthening that
same journey, the result will always be the same: We are not God or
gods; we will not live forever.

Thus, the harmony of which I write is the realization that the
rhythm of our life's journey is a shared one, governed by our own biological time clock. Recognition of this fact is, in and of itself, the
beginning point of any realistic and honest approach to prayer. We
are part of a larger rhythm, a grander vision, a "Divine pattern" if you
will, initiated eons ago, toward what end we know not, though *all*
faith communities attempt to posit certainty of such knowledge on
this very point.

Giving voice to this realization, therefore, the only appropriate
prayer is that of *thanksgiving*—whether or not there is a Deity "out
there" who can hear or respond to that which is uttered. "Thank you,
God, for initiating a process whereby this universe and I came to be

for however long I am to be part of it." Neither false hope nor illusion nor delusion are part of such expression—nor any expectation of response. Instead, the emphasis is properly where it should be: on life itself as the ultimate, albeit temporary, gift of God to humanity.

Having so written, the second premise of a rethought understanding of prayer, that creation allows us more possibilities for human growth than does destruction, follows logically. Even today, with all our advanced knowledge and renewed emphases on the health of our physical selves, we still appear to use only approximately one-seventh of our individual biological capacity and one-seventh of our brain capacity. Contemplating a world where opportunities abound for both individuals and groups to maximize their creative potential results in a second prayer of thanksgiving: "Thank you, God, for endowing me/us with potential yet to be actualized for my own benefit as well as for the benefit of others." Again, response is neither needed or sought. Nor is there any understanding that such words are directed toward nor received by Deity.

Our moral-ethical responsibilities, subsequent to the *Shoah*, are thus self-evident. Having destroyed so much of humanity, Jewish and other, during the years 1939-1945, and along with such "mega-death" of untold human potential, we are mandated, out of our very concern for our own survival as well as the survival of both humanity and spaceship earth to address creative growth possibilities in all areas of human endeavor. Be it psychology or physics, anthropology or astronomy, humanities or science, or religion or faith or what have you—every aspect of human endeavor now needs to be rethought with an eye toward its creative potential for even further growth. Indeed, there is no such thing as an unaskable question; only answers that stifle the very process of questioning and limit our growth potential.

Consistent with this understanding, therefore, is the need to rethink the sociology of groups, all kinds of groups, and the authority structures that govern them and impose their standards of membership. Be they countries and citizenship, religions and faith communities, even fraternal, social or cultural organizations, in light of the diminishing of human potential because of the *Shoah*, the new emphasis of such groups must be inclusive rather than exclusive.

Indeed, this idea of increasing diversity of membership as an aid to present and future creative growth potential flows directly out of the concept of "covenants of dialogue" addressed in Chapter 2. The more dialogues that can be both initiated and sustained within various groups and across group boundaries; and the more diverse those participating in such dialogues can be, the greater will be the possibilities for growth as new thoughts, new ideas, and new experiences are introduced on a repeated and regular basis. We will never know either quantitatively or qualitatively the ideas, dreams, and visions lost during the *Shoah*; they are gone forever. However, we can halt the continual diminishing of our own present and future potential by our affirmation of the opportunities that creation, in all its various manifestations and forms, presents, bound only by our humanity and whatever limits we choose to impose upon ourselves as a result of such dialogues.

A brief word, then, is in order about authority and authority structures. Sociologists draw a distinction between *ascribed* authority by virtue of position or title and *achieved* authority by virtue of effort. *In light of the Shoah, the only authority that exists morally and ethically is that which I as an individual or we as a group willingly give over to others; not that which is taken from us or that which attempts to sustain itself by virtue of its place in the past.* Historically traditional understandings of authority and authority structures are, additionally, a casualty of the *Shoah*; and although this topic will be more fully addressed in Chapter 4, dealing with the dual concepts of *halakhah* (law) and *mitzvot* (commandments), creative human growth potential demands a far freer approach to authority in all aspects of human endeavor that previously thought or understood.

Third, the oft-used cliche "beauty is in the eyes of the beholder" has particular relevance to the concept of prayer suggested in this chapter: that of the verbalization of realities and truths freed from the necessity of a responding Deity. That individuals are diversely capable of appreciating beauty on a variety of levels, intellectual, emotional, physical, spiritual, as well as through the five senses, presents us with yet another opportunity for thanksgiving: "Thank you, God, for initiating a process of life, filled with potential, whereby I am able to appreciate that which is beautiful and which produces pleasure within me." Aestheticism thus becomes intimately bound up with my life affirmation as I now choose to share my concept of the beautiful with others without attempting to force into a "straight jacket" either their thinking or my own. Beautiful words or music or the visual or some combination of the three; my appreciation of the beautiful and my willingness both to share such with my neighbor and have my neighbor share such with me forges yet another link in yet another covenant of dialogue.

By extension, therefore, the worship experience, the actualization of the prayer process, must be freer in its use of any and all artistic forms to "move" the worshipper-participant on those occasions when one enters the sanctuary. Liturgical expression must equally draw upon all the possibilities of human aesthetic endeavor—music, words, dance, the so-called plastic arts—drawing upon both the past and the present in the creation of a meaningful religious future. What was and what is no longer bind the worshipper to what is and what can be in light of the *Shoah*. Again, the consent of the community and not the external imposition of authority validate the experience of worship for the individual worshipper and the group. Similarly, the willingness to continue to be open to experiment and experimental forms of worship sends the only appropriate message to all who care about the experience of worship and prayer in the post-*Shoah* world: "We invite you in to be part of what we are trying to achieve and accomplish in the aftermath of the devastation and destruction caused by the *Shoah*. We are confident and open that your own contributions, too, will be meaningful and significant and received with dignity, respect, and integrity."

Thus, the responsibility of the religiously and aesthetically sensitive Jew or Christian five decades after the *Shoah* is threefold: (1) to *preserve* that from the past which continues to be meaningful in all the ways in which "meaning" can be achieved; (2) to *adapt* those forms capable of adaptation because they contain within them the seeds and kernels of meaningful expression; and (3) to *innovate* where new realities engender new responsibilities; *Yom Ha-Shoah*, Holocaust Remembrance Day, being but the most obvious example, with contemporary gender sensitivity and the rebirth of the State of Israel additional examples. Rethinking both the Jewish life cycle and the Jewish festival cycle, Chapters 5 and 6, expand upon this central and crucial idea.

Fourth, the prayer *words* and prayer *books* of both Jewish and Christian religious traditions must now be properly, appropriately, and appreciatively understood as the poeticized expressions of the generations and *not* as literal statements of either universally accepted or acknowledged religious or theological truths, through some truths may indeed be contained within the various formulations of the prayers. Additionally, they must likewise be understood far more subjectively than heretofore perceived: as the musings of individuals and communities at various historical epochs giving voice to their own beliefs. Consensus understandings of faith transversing the generations does not always imply truth; the *Shoah* itself, sadly and tragically, is, seemingly, the very denial of all such past understandings. And whereas the concerns of these two faith communities may be similar to the point of actually being the same (e.g., life and death, good and evil, war and peace, survival and extinction, holy and ordinary, clean and unclean), and the linguistic formulations both similar and dissimilar, the reality of the *Shoah* demands an "open-endedness" to prayer that is the very opposite of authoritatively imposed dogma. *Paralleling the lack of any support for externally imposed authorities and authority-structures, both dogmatic and creedal formulations as expressed in prayer are no longer valid.* Because of the *Shoah*, it is no longer appropriate to say "*This* is what we believe when we pray," but, rather, "*This* is what past (and some contemporary) generations meant and believed when they prayed these words. May they trigger within me additional thoughts, ideas, feelings, words, expressions as I now attempt to give voice to my own concerns, fears, joys, and the like."

All of this leads to my fifth understanding: that the disciplined gathering of like-minded individuals or groups in celebration and in sorrow can help energize us to confront the challenges of our own day and learn from each other. As has been expressed previously, what is here implied is two things: (1) that, in light of the *Shoah*, all manner of groups must now rethink in much, much more inclusivistic rather than exclusivistic terms than ever before; and (2) that covenants of dialogue freely entered into can enrich all such groups as well as build and strengthen bridges and bonds between groups. One of the primary functions of all religious groups and faith traditions, affirmed by both Jews and Christians and Judaism and Christianity, in all their diverse expressions, is the building up of nurturing and caring groups. In light of the *Shoah*, therefore, we who hurt, be we First, Second, or Third Generation, our families and friends, or those only remotely, indirectly, or even peripherally affected, must be welcomed both by our own communities as well as those we choose to join. Places must be given to us and vehicles provided for us to give voice to our own unique concerns from our own unique vantage point. Although the *Shoah* may, in deed and in truth, be an unwelcome guest at all Jewish and Christian gatherings, those connected to it must not be turned away, ignored, or disenfranchised if we are to learn together, uncomfortable though such learning may ultimately prove to be, and prevent repetition of such nightmarish and ghoulish horror.

Penultimately, this entire discussion of prayer is predicated upon two suppositions: (1) that, for some among us, because of the *Shoah*, the historically traditional understandings of prayer are no longer meaningful and relevant to our lives, though we very much want to pray and participate in religiously centered communities of faith for our own authenticity and self-validation; and (2) that we need not suspend our intellect nor deny the historical reality of the *Shoah* when we engage in prayer. Thus, the alternative understandings of prayer presented in this chapter are an attempt to do both: to suggest to all who continue to struggle with prayer after the *Shoah* that it *is* possible to pray, though never again as those in the past prayed; and that the restlessness of the post-*Shoah* mind and mind set must be given their rightful place in any meaningful discussion of prayer.

The last question that now must be raised is "Why?" Why bother with prayer at all? Why bother to be part of any so-named praying community? Despite the overwhelming impact of the *Shoah*, the "poetry of the soul" continues to assert itself. Despite our all-too-ready willingness to engage in despair, life itself and its singularly unique "moments of beauty" continue to present themselves even to the most affected and afflicted. Short of permanent institutional residence and mental and physical impotence, survivors and their children, scholars, and friends continue to go on with life. Suicide for the vast majority of those addressed in this book is simply *not* an option. We children of survivors, we Second Generation, *are* born into a community, primarily of Jews, and wish to remain so. That some among us are no longer comfortable with the historically traditional understandings of faith and religion because of the *Shoah* comes as no surprise to anyone. That we wish to enter into on-going dialogue with our fellow Jews about God, covenant, prayer, and so forth should be interpreted and understood as our *positive* response, not to the *Shoah* itself, but rather to meaningful and creative Jewish religious survival and our determination to enlist others, Jews and Christians, in preventing its repetition.

That said, we turn next to the very essence of the Jewish religious experience: that of *halakhah* and *mitzvot*, law and commandments. For this Second Generation thinker, no longer accepting of such as Divinely given, can there be any other interpretation and understanding that accords discipline its rightful and appropriate place within the Jewish panoply of ideas and charts the way Jews can now *do* their Judaism five decades after the *Shoah*?

Note

1. Significantly, it seems to me, scientific thinkers are beginning to ask *religious* and *theological* questions; a number of books in my library bear witness to that fact. On the other hand, however, we religious and theological thinkers are not yet conversant enough with the literature to begin asking appropriate *scientific* questions. Here is yet another area worthy of further exploration and thought.

4

Halakhah and *Mitzvot*:
Law and Commandments—
The Heart of the Matter[1]

For me, in light of everything thus far written, as should be patently obvious, the understanding of God as "Commander" is no longer applicable, and therefore, the understanding of "commandment" emanating from that God equally no longer applicable. Except for the exigencies of history that continue to deny us Jews any opportunity to escape our Jewish identity, the only "commandments" that exist—if, indeed, it is even right and proper to use such a term—are those we would willingly and positively take upon ourselves out of our desire to be positively affirming Jews. (Might the same, therefore, not also be said of our Christian brothers and sisters?)

At the very heart of both the historically traditional and contemporary Jewish religious movements is the notion of *mitzvah* or "commandment" as the Jewishly obligated act in response to the "call" of the *Mitzaveh* or "Commander." Having tentatively and painfully rethought such notions of God, covenant, and prayer in response to the *Shoah*, to continue to maintain such an historically traditional notion of *mitzvah*, it seems to me, not only beggars the question, but negates the historical realities of the *Shoah* itself. The classical understanding of *mitzvah* is, itself, an affirmation of a relationship no longer extent, *if ever*, and likewise, a casualty of the *Shoah*. That God calls, we respond through *mitzvot*, and God, in turn, responds to us is no longer credible. Emil Fackenheim's highly touted "commanding voice at Auschwitz," heard only by those who are already listening, will *not* be heard by those already sensitized or not so sensitized to their Jewish and Christian responsibilities and obligations because of events of the *Shoah*. In addition, even Fackenheim himself would not have the temerity to maintain that this voice is the *Bat Kol* or "Divine voice" of talmudic tradition, which seemingly spoke to the Rabbis in the ancient academies so very long ago. Thus the notion of *mitzvah* as the religiously and Jewishly commanded act of God to Jewish creation primarily imposed upon the Jewish people by a historically bound and committed Authority and rabbinic authority structure is, truly, yet another victim of the *Shoah*.[2]

In light of the preceding, then, having now, sadly, rejected the understanding of God as *Mitzaveh*, "Commander," the question remains: "What criteria or standards can and do we use to incorporate into our Jewish and Christian lives those ritual-ceremonial and moral-ethical behaviors we need to find them meaningful, even if we no longer regard them as commandments?" And, secondarily for some, primarily for others, "Why do we even choose to do so?"

If we are honest and truthful with ourselves, fully recognizing the painful difficulty inherent in the task, there are only six criteria: (1) intellectual, (2) aesthetic, (3) emotional, (4) physical, (5) psychological, and (6) spiritual. Though obviously spelled out in more specific detail in Chapter 5, dealing with the Jewish life cycle, and Chapter 6, dealing with the Jewish festival cycle, what now follows is an expansion and explication of these six criteria, the very framework in which these subsequent two chapters make sense. Without this coherent framework of understanding, therefore, religious and theological anarchy will result, governed only by the most specious kind of subjectivity, a topic to which we shall return after delineating these criteria. Specific examples and applications will be the foci of the next two chapters.

As was the case in the previous chapter dealing with prayer in light of the *Shoah*, it is imperative not to suspend one's intellectual gifts when addressing religious behaviors of both the ritual-ceremonial and moral-ethical kind. *If it makes sense to me, if I can understand it, given my education and training, if I can appreciate it on this initial level of logical thought taking into consideration my own human experiences to this point, then I am prepared both to accept and to practice such Jewish ritual and ethical behaviors as are in accord with my own understanding of my self and my relationship to the Jewish people.* The starting point for any contemporary commitment to Jewish doing, however defined, therefore, in the aftermath of the *Shoah*, is the individual Jew rather than the Jewish group. Communal loyalty and commitment, in the absence of any authorities and authority structures, now begins with the individual being welcomed into the group, zealously protective of his or her freedom to say "No!" at certain moments and not being afraid of being expelled from the group.

Two additional points flow from this initial understanding: One, that the threefold responsibility to preserve, to adapt, and to innovate is central in any discussion of Jewish doing after the *Shoah*; and, two, that such a commitment to Jewish doing requires a life-long adult-level commitment to Jewish study, long a hallmark of the Jewish religious tradition. Informed, knowledgable decision making resulting in Jewish doing may very well come closer to any semblance of "commandment" after the *Shoah* than anything else, even taking into consideration and appreciation the very subjective nature of this entire discussion. "I will do Jewish *X* because it is in accord with my own understanding" or "I will not do Jewish *X* because it is not in accord with my own understanding" must now be accepted by both the Jewish individual and Jewish people after the *Shoah*, without penalty, realizing that just as individuals change, so, too, do ideas and ideals change, and that the seriously committed Jew may very well evolve one set of Jewish behaviors now only to disregard any or all of them and recast them all over again. What remains crucial, therefore, is the willingness of the Jewish people to provide a place, a home, for the post-*Shoah* individual in quest of a "Judaism that makes sense."

Second, even more subjective than the intellectual when it comes to Jewish doing after the *Shoah*, is the aesthetic; that is, that which results in or produces a pleasurable experience for the individual or group. Recognizing only too well that the cliche "beauty is in the eyes of the beholder," both individually and collectively, remains a truism, Jewish behavior must now incorporate into its doing that which evokes aesthetic pleasure of both a positive and negative kind even if I am unable to fully explain my rationale for its doing. "I like doing Jewish *X* because it gives me pleasure, and, therefore, I will continue to do it," or "I dislike doing Jewish *X* because it does not evoke pleasure within me, and, therefore, I will not or will no longer do it" must be accepted by the individual free of guilt and by the group free of negative response.

Paralleling the discussion of the last chapter, aesthetic appreciation, too, requires a willingness to open doors to human creativity; that what was acceptable in a previous generation may or may not be so today, especially in the area of Jewish ritual-ceremonial behavior. Not only do generational standards change, but even within a generation. What is, therefore, demanded is that same willingness to experiment, to try, to accept, and to reject, personally and collectively.

In line, therefore, with this second criteria for the evaluation of Jewish doing in the aftermath of the *Shoah* is an appreciation of the emotional component of the individual without denigrating or exploit-

ing it in the context of Jewish behaviors. Just as the doing of specially Jewish acts may produce within me aesthetic pleasure, so, too,
will the doing of these same or other Jewish acts evoke an emotional
response from me, laughter, tears, and so on. Indeed, for the post-
Shoah individual, recognition of a heightened awareness of emo-
tionality may very well be a factor in behavior: The continuous
absence of family members throughout one's life, and the retelling of
absentee stories referred to in the Introduction, may very well produce an emotional vulnerabilty not yet fully explored in the context of
Jewish doing. My own father's inability to wear the traditional skullcap
(*yarmulke* or *kippah*), for example, as too painful a reminder of his
own Orthodox Jewish past in Germany, may result in his own son's
desire to wear a *kippah* as my own affirmation of my Jewish self
when engaged in Jewish doing.

Then, too, the doing of certain Jewish behaviors, both ritual-
ceremonial and moral-ethical, evoke from me a certain physical
response that, in turn, becomes rationale enough for their continued
doing or the reverse. Indeed, this very discussion of Jewish behavior
is cognizant of the very physicality of Jewish acts: that although they
may start in either the mind or the "heart," their very activity is in the
realm of the physical. The lifting of the Torah scroll at appropriate
times, for example, is a physical act, yet one that may likewise evoke
an emotionally positive response from me because of any already-
committed intellectual position. All *acts* involve the physical, and
recognition of their importance as a valid criterion for their continued
Jewish doing or nondoing after the *Shoah* now becomes paramount.

At this juncture, too, it is equally important to note, as indicated
earlier, that the criteria laid out thus far interweave in the doing of various Jewish behaviors. Certain acts may be accepted or rejected based
on one or more criteria; others may be accepted or rejected based on
the interplay of those same criteria. What governs these criteria, then,
significantly enough, is not their intellectual appreciation, their emotional warmth, or their physical pleasure, but the *Shoah* itself. It now
becomes the overriding standard with which to evaluate all manner of
doing, Jewish and otherwise. "In light of the *Shoah* . . . do I do or not
do *A* or non-*A*?"

Likewise, in the aftermath of the *Shoah*, whatever psychological
needs I may have, in turn, become criteria with which to evaluate
Jewish doing. The need to verbalize positively and negatively feelings both positive and negative, the need for companionship and
community, the need for safety and security in the post-*Shoah* world,
the need to be allowed to grow intellectually, freed from past con-

straints without feeling threatened early on by tentative conclusions, continue to focus my attention on Jewish behavior. Psychologically, the prior dependence on the *Mitzaveh* as the "Commanding Presence" demanding of me performance of Jewish acts no longer makes sense in this world beyond the *Shoah*. Thus, the acts themselves are no longer commanded and must now be reevaluated using these five criteria plus one more.

All Jewish acts may be assessed from a variety of perspectives, including those already enumerated, as well as their historical or agricultural origins, but what frames their doing is the spiritual or religious nature of the acts themselves. The question then becomes whether or not such acts possess within themselves the possibilities of raising me to a new level of awareness of reality, a higher *madrega* if you will. "Do these acts make me a better person in a moral-ethical sense now that the *Shoah* has taken place?" "Do these acts root me in a place from which I can grow as a human being?" "Do these acts enable me to continue my life's journey freed from much of the pain of the past and minimizing much of the pain of the present?"

I will paraphrase what I have written on a previous occasion. Admittedly, these six criteria for the observance of any and all so-called *mitzvot* or commandments are subjective. But honestly recognized subjectivity is all that remains in light of what transpired now almost one-half century ago. *The reality of our world is that there is no longer any authority or authority structure, other than that to which we would willingly subject ourselves, which has any authority over us.*

Admittedly, these six criteria are selective in that sense that I, or anyone else, select from the ever-growing body of Jewish resource literature, which begins with Torah, Mishnah, and Talmud and includes the various categories of *mitzvot*, "commandments," those that give meaning to life itself. Thus, the only *mitzvah*, "commandment," required now is that of study. Because neither I nor anyone else can command observance of *mitzvot*, the responsibility of observance falls directly upon the shoulders of the individual to decide for oneself what one would willingly choose to observe. Such a mature and responsible recognition of the freedom to be and to do in this post-*Shoah* world requires an equally mature commitment to study those same resources in order to make meaningfully informed decisions. To refuse to do so and to refuse to study is not Jewish freedom but Jewish stupidity. It is, equally, to reduce being Jewish to some sort of quasi-biological status; and that notion the Nazis themselves carried out to its logical and horrifying conclusion.

Secondarily, the question raised early on in this chapter, "Why bother to set any standards whatsoever for Jewish behavior?" now demands an answer. The affirmation of my Jewish self discussed earlier in this book is manifested concretely in Jewish doing. The next two chapters permit me to reinterpret the two categories of Jewish doing—the life cycle and the festival cycle—in ways that now make sense to me after the *Shoah*. This discussion of standards and evaluative criteria for Jewish doing is the rationale behind what follows. More significant, however, I remain committed to the idea that Judaism, no longer presented in an historically traditional way, provides the individual Jew as well as the collective Jewish people with a way to travel forward on the journey of life, to meet its challenges and surmount its obstacles, and to receive whatever blessings life has in store. I remain equally committed to the idea that that same Judaism, now reinterpreted, can continue to speak meaningfully to a generation transformed by the horrors of the *Shoah* and to a world no longer what it was, altered irrevocably in ways we have only begun to explore and understand. Though I fully believe there is no blessing in tragedy and suffering, though we may experience the nobility of the human person in the process, out of such wrestling with the meaning of tragedy and suffering can come a renewed energy to avoid the mistakes of the past and create both a present and a future profoundly different from that past.

Logically, therefore, from this initial discussion of the *mitzvot*, "commandments," we turn next to a discussion of *halakhah*, the disciplined system of Jewish law that has sustained our Jewish people since the Pharisaic-early Rabbinic period and continues to be the raison d'être for much of contemporary Judaism and Jewish practice.

Ultimately, there are only two ways to perceive the experience of Judaism in the religio-spiritual context of what we may call the Divine-human encounter: Either Judaism comes directly from God through the medium of revelation called *Torah* and authoritatively interpreted and reinterpreted by designated spokes*men* (Rabbis) through a binding authority structure (*halakhah* or Jewish law) and willingly affirmed by the community of Jews in each and every generation; or Judaism is the evolving response of the Jewish people in each and every generation to its own changing perception of this encounter and the historical cross-currents that continually modify what the past has wrought. If the latter is in fact a true and accurate representation of reality, as I obviously believe it is, then the question of authority, always central and crucial, is understood differently by different generations, but also willingly affirmed by those who wish to do so.

For those for whom Judaism is a God-given gift, the *Shoah*, too, must be, somehow, incorporated into the overall schema as must all historical events and phenomena. The halakhic or Jewish legal system is a binding, authoritative system of Jewish doing that raises no questions of meaning nor entertains the possibilities of certain events and historical happenstance falling outside the Divine purview. The proper and appropriate *Jewish* response to the vagaries and complexities of our world is contained in and evidenced by adherence to the system itself that, like Scripture itself, came directly from God. The so-called Oral Law (*Torah sheb'al peh*), in the eyes of the Rabbis and those who accord them authority, possesses all the force of the so-called Written Law (*Torah shebichtav*), oft-times surpassing it in the ingenuity of its legal pronouncements.

Yet, this disciplined approach to religious and ethical behavior as detailed by the *halakhah* should not be minimized as to either the sincerity of its followers and expositors or its contribution to Jewish survival. It has withstood both the historical test of time and triumphed over all previous onslaughts against it. What is at issue, however, is not the need for self-evident discipline in the doing of Judaism, but, rather, the Divine rationale behind it as well as the positing of certain authorities and interpretations as the *only* legitimate forms of Jewish development and growth.

In light of everything I have written thus far, no longer can we say that *halakhah*, the Jewish legal system, comes from a God who was silent-absent-indifferent-incapable of responding during the *Shoah*. That God interacted with us and gave us the *halakhah* but did nothing in our so recent past raises all over again the very questions that are the substance of this book.

The *halakhah*, therefore, is a humanly interpretive system of Judaism, inspired by love of the Divine, based on the very real need for this distinctive community to survive. Its genius is that it has addressed every aspect of human endeavor in a practical, logical, systematic manner, subject to its own rules, expanding and contracting as circumstances warrant. *But it is not Divine.* That, sadly, is one of the all-too-clear lessons of the *Shoah*, for it, too, possessed little to enable too, too few of us to survive the Nazis. To be sure, it did provide comfort and solace to and for some among those who stood at the abyss and ultimately were pushed into it. *But it is not Divine.*

At its best, it is law by the consent of the governed. No longer can we say that those who disregard it or choose to ignore it will be punished severely at some distant point in the future. No longer can we say that those who did not live under it during the years 1933(39)-1945, or abandoned it altogether, were punished because of their seeming disregard of it. No longer can we say that those who lived under it were "saved" by it in the most literal sense of the word. The price paid was far too great for anyone to see the *Shoah* in such narrowly particularistic Jewish terms.

No longer is it morally and religiously creditable after the *Shoah* to argue and maintain that Judaism for the survivors, however defined, can be interpreted and understood in only one way, that of the halakhic legal system. No longer is it morally and religiously defensible after the *Shoah* to argue and maintain that only those schooled in the halakhic manner of interpreting Judaism, that of Talmud and Midrash, are the true and authentic representative spokes*men* for the Jewish religious tradition. Such consideration returns us to an earlier notion of exclusivistic rather than inclusivistic thinking and demeans the surviving Jewish people. The Rabbis of the halakhic part of the Jewish religious tradition are the authentic spokesmen for those to and for whom they are the authentic spokesmen. But Judaism is not monolithic, nor are the Jewish people monolithic. Nor has it or have we ever been so. What remains valid in the aftermath of the *Shoah* are all manners of interpretation that groups of Jews affirm as valid for themselves: Reform, Conservative, Orthodox, Reconstructionist, Humanist, Secularist, Zionist, and others yet to be created. Judaism is what it has always been: the creation of the Jewish people in all its many and varied forms. What now becomes paramount after the *Shoah* is the building of intracommunal bridges between and among the various subgroups of Jews.

What has just been written is not a defense nor a rationale of nonhalakhic forms of Judaism in terms of their own presentations of themselves. Rather, it is to state most emphatically that the *Shoah* itself has destroyed for ever and all time any notion whatsoever of one authentic manner of Jewish expression and, with it, any notion of one particular group of spokes*men* as the only authentic spokespersons. Today, whatever theologies or philosophies of Judaism attract Jews and win allegiance to their banners are true and valid for those Jews who choose to be part of their group. And, although intragroup rivalry may occupy an honored place within the historical sweep of the Jewish people, after the *Shoah*, the noun *Jew* is far more important than any adjective whatsoever.

We turn now to the first practical working out of this post-*Shoah* Jewish theology: that of rethinking the Jewish life cycle.

Notes

1. Ultimately, there are only *two* ways to perceive the Jewish religious tradition: either it is a legally mandated system of religious discipline emanating directly from God at Sinai, with the Torah interpreted correctly only by authoritative spokes*men* or it is not. The former position is that of the Orthodox; the latter that of the Reform and Reconstructionists, with the Conservatives occupying the "space" between the two.

2. Perhaps the best introduction to Fackenheim's thought is that edited by Michael L. Morgan of Indiana University: *The Jewish Thought of Emil Fackenheim: A Reader* (Detroit: Wayne State University Press, 1987).

5

Rethinking the Jewish Life Cycle: From Birth to Death

Celebration of life-cycle events must now be rethought because of the *Shoah*, not so much for the specific manner in which they are celebrated, but for the rationale behind their celebration. For some among us, no longer can this or that life-cycle event be celebrated or sanctified for the historically traditional reasons previously supplied. Though the actual practices themselves may not vary one iota from previous patterns of behavior, the "whys" and "wherefores" in light of the *Shoah* now demand a degree of intellectual consistency, coupled with theological integrity, not necessarily required in Judaism's and Christianity's long past. No longer can the ritual of *Brith Milah*, the "covenant of circumcision" of an eight-day-old Jewish boy, for example, now be understood as his parents' entering that infant into a covenant directly with God, when some among those already committed to that covenant realized its impotence throughout Nazi-occupied Europe and transmitted such, oft-times not in words but in feelings and expressions, to their offspring and beyond. To continue such notions only perpetuates the pain. New words are needed to address new realities; if not new words, then new interpretations of old words, not for all, but certainly for those among us for whom the old ways can no longer be maintained or resurrected because of the historically traditional reasons previously given.

The life's journey shared by all humanity, regardless of faith community, is the same. What separates us from the lowered ordered species of the animal kingdom is our ability to "mark the moments" of the journey in celebration or in sorrow. It is, therefore, to the enduring credit of all historic faith communities, and evidence of their continuing genius, that the carefully crafted rituals and ceremonies created for these moments have found responsive audiences in their communities, despite specifically changing practices over the course of the centuries. The reality of the *Shoah* and any attempt to live in a post-*Shoah* religious world neither denies nor denigrates the need for these moments. It is the rationale behind their celebration that is challenged by the *Shoah*.

Generally speaking, the journey is as follows: There is (1) birth, (2) growth, (3) maturation, (4) decay, and (5) death. Jewishly speaking, there is (1) birth: *Brith Milah* (covenant of circumcision), naming, *Pidyon ha-Ben* (redemption of the first-born son), and adoption; (2) growth: consecration, *Bar* and *Bat Mitzvah*, confirmation, and graduation; (3) maturation: betrothal, wedding and marriage and notable anniversaries, birthing and family, *Hanukkat ha-Bayit* (dedication of new home), and conversion; (4) decay: aging and sickness, death of parents, and divorce; and (5) death: confession and dying, and funeral and *Yahrtzeit* (anniversary of death).

The pragmatic working out of these various life-cycle rituals and ceremonies, both liturgically and theologically, is contained in the rabbinical manuals of the three major American Jewish religious movements: Orthodox, Conservative, and Reform.[1] They are *Hamadrikh: A Rabbi's Guide* (Orthodox); *Likutei Tefillah:A Rabbi's Manual* (Conservative); and *Rabbi's Manual* or *Ma'agele Tsedek: Rabbi's Manual* (Reform).[2] Therefore, a close examination of these four volumes should yield, if properly understood, the theological rationale behind the celebration of these various life-cycle events and whether or not there is any discernible impact whatsoever of the *Shoah* upon these events. It is to them and to the events themselves that we now turn.

Birth: *Brith Milah*, Naming, *Pidyon ha-Ben*, and Adoption

According to the Orthodox, either the *mohel* (ritual circumcisor) or father recites an introductory blessing containing the words "the precept which the Creator, praised be He, commanded me/us" (p. 33), momentarily followed by the formulaic blessing "who hast sanctified us with Thy commandments and enjoined us [literally, "and commanded us"] the rite of circumcision" (p. 34). After the actual circumcision has been completed, the blessing reads "who hast sanctified us by Thy commandments and hast bidden us to make him enter into the covenant of Abraham our father" (p. 34). Included in the accompanying wine blessing are the words "deliver from destruction the dearly beloved of our flesh, for the sake of the covenant Thou hast set in our bodies" (p. 35). Significantly, the Torahitic verses included are the following:

> He hath remembered His covenant for ever, the word which He commanded to a thousand generations; [the covenant] which made with Abraham, and His oath unto Isaac, and confirmed the same unto Jacob for a statute, to Israel for an everlasting covenant. . . . And Abraham circumcised his son Isaac when he was eight days old, as God commanded him. (p. 36)

Additional blessings are offered and preparations are then made for the meal celebration.

The Conservative ritual includes the initial three blessings cited previously, modifying the text ever so slightly, but *not* with regard to the *Brith Milah* being a "commanded act" of Deity (pp. 9-10).

Oddly enough, the Reform Movement, a distinctly nonhalakhic Jewish religious movement, includes both "commandment blessings" (pp. 9-10) and an additional Torahitic verse in the first of its two rabbis' manuals:

> For He established a testimony in Jacob, and appointed a law in Israel, which He commanded to our fathers, that they should make them known to their children; that the generations to come might know them, even the children that should be born. (p. 10)

In the newer of the two manuals, a "creative service" is included in which those assembled play a significant role, echoing initially such phrases as "the *Berit*, the Covenant between God and the Jewish people" (p. 6) and "May we, like our ancestor Abraham, obey the commandment . . ." (p. 7). Previous Torahitic passages are likewise offered (p. 10), as well as the formulaic "commanded" blessing (p. 11).

Nowhere in any of these three *Brith Milah* rituals, Orthodox, Conservative or Reform, is there any indication of the impact of the *Shoah* upon the life of the Jewish parents or Jewish family. Likewise, the very issues with which this book is concerned, God, covenant, prayer, *halakhah*, and *mitzvot*, are equally not addressed. What then are survivors of the *Shoah* and their children to do if they can no longer accept the collective rationale behind this initial act of Jewish doing and commitment (i.e., God commanded *Brith Milah* and therefore we do it) but very much want to remain part and parcel of the Jewish people and the Jewish faith community? It seems to me there are two seeds, history and tradition, both of which are already contained in the previously described ceremonies.

For better than 2,000 years, despite all the injustices wrought by history, Jewish parents have chosen to affirm their Jewish selves and their male offspring by the religious ritual of *Brith Milah* accompanying the physical-surgical procedure. "We are Jews and we make that affirmatively positive Jewish commitment that we want our son to initially live his own life as a Jew." Honestly recognizing this, the force of that historical commitment carries with it a certain moral suasion that is no less pervasive today in the aftermath of the *Shoah* that it was prior to it.

Equally, the force of better than 2,000 years of a religious tradition as the way in which Jews "mark this moment" carries with it its own sanctity. This is the "Jewish way" to do Judaism. By so doing, Jews enter into covenants with other Jews and with the Jewish people as a collectivity, covenanting not only with Abraham but with Abraham's descendants, vowing here to work together for the betterment of our Jewish people by "contributing" yet another "worker" toward the realization of our ages-old dream of *Shalom*, peace for all humankind. Again, nothing here would be problematic for those no longer accepting of or comfortable with historically traditional explanations in light of the *Shoah*.

What is rejected is any notion of God as *Mitzaveh*, Commander, the act of *Brith Milah* as *mitzvah*, commandment, and the parents as *mitzuvim*, commanded. This conscious decision to do with a newly supplied rationale for doing, based in part upon the emphases of the past to preserve, adapt, and innovate, does honor both to the Jewish religious tradition and to the reality of the meaning of the *Shoah* and does not ignore either. The ceremonies themselves may very well, therefore and however, have to be rewritten.

Neither the Orthodox nor the Conservative nor the initial Reform offering provides a religious ritual for the welcoming of a daughter into the Jewish people. To be sure, all offer prayers upon the birth of a daughter to be shared in the synagogue. Again, no evidence exists as to the impact of the reality of the *Shoah* upon these prayers.

The newer Reform manual does provide a "Covenant Service for a Daughter" (pp. 16-24), paralleling in many ways the aforementioned creative "Covenant Service for a Son" (pp. 6-15). Here, too, the ritual speaks of a covenant entered into (at Sinai) between the Jewish People and God (p. 17) with a formulaic blessing that reads: "We praise You, Adonai our God, Ruler of the universe, who hallows us with *mitzvot* and commands us to bring our daughter into the Covenant of our people, Israel" (pp. 20-21).

Though public celebration of the birth of a daughter is post-Torahitic, and contemporary expressions of equality have had an impact, the very same understanding and reinterpretation of *Brith Milah* holds for the survivors and their children who now wish to affirm the sanctity of this third generation, with obvious modification.

The birth of children, both male and female, is to be celebrated inclusivistically rather an exclusivistically. Jewish parents commit themselves and their children to living Jewish lives by Jewishly "marking the moment." In so doing, they enter into covenants with their fellow Jews for the benefit of all. Nowhere is the emphasis that of the past, of commanded religious obligation being the raison d'être of present and future Jewish behavior. The *Shoah* itself, given its very reality, has proclaimed that understanding at its end.

Pidyon ha-Ben, redemption of the first born son from priestly obligation in exchange for "five shekels of silver," is based on a Torahitic passage from *Shemot* (Exodus) and is applicable only to the first-born Israelite, not to either the *Cohanim* (Priests} or *Leviim* (Levites): "Sanctify unto Me all the first-born, whatsoever openeth the womb among the children of Israel, both of man and of beast, it is Mine" (*Shemot* 13:2).

This passage is included verbatim in the Orthodox ritual (p. 52), following which both the words of the *Cohain* and the Father contain the phrase "as thou art / I am obligated to do according to the Law" (ibid.). The commanded "blessing of obligation" is then offered: "Praised be Thou, O Lord our God, King of the universe, who hast sanctified us by Thy commandments, and hast bidden us [literally, 'and commanded us'] to redeem the first-born son" (ibid.).

The Conservative ritual likewise includes the Torahitic passages from *Bamidbar* (Numbers) 18:16 and *Shemot* (Exodus) 13:2 (p. 15) as well as the aforementioned blessing (p. 16). Both rituals include prayers for God's beneficent guidance of the redeemed one-month-old son.

The Reform movement, historically committed to the complete and total equality of all Jews, male and female, *Cohain*, Levite, and Israelite, provides no ceremony or ritual whatsoever, either in the first or second rabbi's manual.

Again, here, too, the impact of the *Shoah* is nonexistent.[3] Priestly obligation to serve God in light of the *Shoah* is extremely problematic, to say the very least. For those who wish to affirm the celebration that comes with the birth of the first-born, inclusivistically now either a son or a daughter, the whole matter needs be rethought. No longer does it make sense to speak of one being "redeemed from Divine service" after the *Shoah* when the commitment of those already redeemed came to nought. Better to rethink and recreate a liturgical experience along the lines of affirming a commitment to serve the Jewish people and its ongoing quest for survival now than any notion whatsoever of "redemption from" anything. Better still, in light of the *Shoah*, to rethink not only the rationale behind such a ceremonial experience as *Pidyon ha-Ben* but its very practice as well. Courageous confrontation, perhaps, demands that now we question even the very applicability of such a moment as relevant and meaningful to a post-*Shoah* and post-Auschwitz Jewish world. I am more and more inclined to think not.

For those unable to have children, the joy of adoption is boundless. For both Orthodox and Conservative Judaism, in the main, the ritual practices for both male and female as described previously would be applicable. Therefore, the criticism of these expressions is equally applicable. After the *Shoah*, to speak of God as *Mitzaveh*, Commander, Jewish behavior as *mitzvot*, commandments, and the newly adoptive parents as *mitzuvim*, commanded, cannot be affirmed with any clarity of conscience.

The newer Reform rabbi's manual includes two ceremonies for the "Adoption of an Infant" (pp. 25-31) and the "Adoption of an Older Child" (pp. 32-36), both of which contain a series of poetic prayers seeking Divine blessing and offering thanksgiving. Other than the obvious difficulty of asking Divine blessing, here, too, the impact of the *Shoah* is nowhere to be found. Here, too, more thought needs to be put into such experiences, incorporating the excitement of adoption, the need to "mark the moment," the desire to be positively affirming Jews in a world without a Divine Commanding Authority and externally imposed authority structures, and the reality of the *Shoah*. Here, too, the wrestling that remains at the core of this book over the questions of God, covenant, and prayer after the *Shoah* needs to be reflected in any and all of these "birthing rituals." These two ceremonies do, however, show possibilities.

Growth: Consecration, Bar and Bat Mitzvah, Confirmation, and Graduation

"Consecration" marking the children's beginning of formal Jewish education is a creative ceremony of both the "liberal" Conservative and Reform movements, as well as the Reconstructionist movement, appended to the celebration of the festival of *Simchat*

Torah ("Joy of the Torah") at the end of *Sukkot* ("Festival of Booths"). Usually included are both prayers and blessings by both the rabbi and congregation as well as a "group affirmation" by the young people themselves, either kindergarteners or first graders, more often than not the recitation of the *Sh'ma*.[4] It is not found in any of the rabbinical manuals cited. Thus, the aforementioned concerns expressed both in this chapter as well as throughout this book with regard to God, covenant, prayer, *halakhah*, and *mitzvot* are echoed here: The reality of the *Shoah* demands that we think both seriously and creatively as we, following the birth rituals, again commit our young people positively to Judaism and the Jewish people, past, present, and future.

The "coming of age" ritual of Bar Mitzvah (literally, "son of the commandment") for a Jewish boy aged 13 plus one day and the newer ceremony of Bat Mitzvah ("daughter of the commandment") for a Jewish girl age 12 plus one day are, in truth, "additions" to the conduct of the regular Shabbat, festival, or new month worship services by having the young person himself (Orthodox only) or herself (Conservative, Reform, Reconstructionist) conduct part or all of the worship service, reading both Torah and *Haftarah* selections, and delivering a speech. Unique to the Jewish people is this manner of marking the transitional moment from children through puberty to adulthood.

A prayer for the Bar Mitzvah is found in *Hamadrikh* (p. 54) and readings and prayers for both Bar and Bat Mitzvah in *Likutei Tephillah* (pp. 19-20). None whatsoever is found in either Reform rabbis' manuals.

The impact of the *Shoah* is nonexistent here, too, whereas the affirmation of God is that of the historical-traditional understanding. Again, the concerns of this book vis-à-vis God, covenant, prayer, *halakhah*, and *mitzvot* are not addressed.

Also, terminologically, the very use of the term *mitzvah* is equally problematic for the post-*Shoah* Jew who wishes to make a positive commitment of inclusion but rejects this frame of reference to *Mitzaveh-mitzvah-mitzuvim*, Commander-commandment-commanded. Although others may appeal to other terms, perhaps, *now* our "best" label may be *Ben Am Yehudi* or *Bat Am Yehudi*, that is, "son" or "daughter of the Jewish people."[5] And although the very process of this coming of age in the Jewish community, that of preparation for worship and leading-participating in the worship experience, can indeed take into consideration the *Shoah* concerns raised here, obvious modification to the worship service itself would be required but need not be addressed at this point. Chapter 6,

"Rethinking the Festival Cycle: The Calendar in Question," deals with these very issues.

The liberal innovation of "Confirmation," marking the end of the formal supplemental religious education, usually around *Shavuot* ("Festival of Weeks") coinciding with the idea of the "giving of the Torah" by Moses as God's representative at Sinai, for ninth or tenth graders in Reform, Conservative, and Reconstructionist communities has no equivalency in the Orthodox tradition. No prayers, readings, or ceremonies are found in any of the rabbinical manuals, Orthodox, Conservative, or Reform. These celebrations, however, governed only by congregational traditions, are, in the main, "creative services" and, thus, admit the most potential to be forthright in responding to the *Shoah* and its aftermath.

Graduation from high school, "leaving the nest" for the next stage of one's education and growth, be it college or university, trade or vocational schooling, military service or the work force, has not been liturgically addressed by *any* of the Jewish religious movements. Realistically, the leaving of the first-born as well as that of the "last-born" are significant, at times traumatic, moments, filled with hope and concern.[6] Here, too, like Confirmation, is an area and arena worthy of exploration, taking fully into consideration all of the historical, psychological, spiritual motivations of an ages-old religious tradition as well as the reality of the *Shoah*. Sensitive and creative liturgists need now to respond to what has heretofore been a Jewishly missed opportunity.

Maturation: Betrothal, Wedding and Marriage
and Notable Anniversaries, Birthing and Family,
Hanukkat ha-Bayit, and Conversion

The Orthodox rabbi's manual *Hamadrikh* includes only the "correct" form of the *Tenaim* or engagement contract with no attendant blessings or ceremonies (pp. 2-4). The Conservative rabbi's manual *Likutei Tephillah* offers no contract but two prayers and the Scriptural verses of *Shir ha-Shirim* (Song of Songs) 8:6-7 (pp. 30-31). The Reform *Rabbi's Manual* offers one prayer (p. 23) and *Ma'agele Tsedek* offers two prayers (pp. 46-47). All of the prayers ask God's blessing upon the couple to be married. Nowhere is the impact of the *Shoah* in evidence. Again, creative opportunities exist within all three movements, as well as the Reconstructionists, for an affirmatively positive liturgical expression for a couple to commit themselves and their future to the Jewish people, well aware of the past and the impact and implications of the *Shoah*.

The Orthodox wedding service (pp. 15-22) includes a series of blessings of God and the couple including wine, the recital of vows or oaths, the giving to the bride of the ring, the reading of the *Ketubah* or wedding contract, as well s the understanding of a certain sense of "commanded obligations" in the marital relationship. The Conservative wedding service (pp. 32-48) is essentially this same format.

The Reform *Rabbi's Manual* offers three "marriage services" (pp. 24-28, 29-34, 35-39), along the same general outline, in contradistinction to only one for both Orthodox and Conservative, with one significant addition and one significant subtraction: All three have parallel expressions for the exchange of wedding rings, based on the Reform principle of the equality of men and women, as opposed to the historical Jewish tradition whereby a wedding ring was given only to the bride. Nowhere, however, is provision made in any ceremony for the "reading of the *Ketubah*."

Ma'agele Tsedek offers four "wedding services" (pp. 50-59, 60-68, 69-76, 77-84), maintains the equality of men and women during the exchange of rings and *does* provide a place for the reading of the *Ketubah* in all four services. Both manuals, like their Orthodox and Conservative counterparts, offer blessings to and from God and to and for the couple.

Again, as has so often been the case with all of these life-cycle moments, the impact of the *Shoah* appears nonexistent and the concerns raised equally are not addressed. Opportunities to positively affirm a Jewish tomorrow, despite a horrendous yesterday that will not allow us to forget or ignore the *Shoah* and be liturgically creative and consistent and responsible still await expression.

All four manuals offer special prayers of thanksgiving and continued blessing to God for special wedding anniversaries, silver (25) and gold (50) (Orthodox, pp. 90-91; Conservative, pp. 51-55; Reform I, pp. 46-49; Reform II, pp. 87-95). Both the Conservative and Reform offer additional brief ceremonies to highlight the occasions.

In light of the *Shoah* and the concerns addressed in Chapter 1, "The Problem with God," and Chapter 3, "The Crises of Prayer," does it any longer make sense to appeal to such a God, even on these happiest of occasions? Is, after the *Shoah*, the mouthing of such words little more than platitude and poetic rhetoric? The joy of marriage and significant anniversaries *can* be celebrated within the Jewish community and Jewish religious tradition. Indeed, now, both *must* be celebrated by the contemporary Jewish religious communities. But ignoring the philosophical and theological implications of the absence of God during the *Shoah* and fruitless appeals for succor and relief during those dark years does not dismiss them out of hand because the occasions are now happy ones. Better to make positive, honest affirmation and include in our thinking and renewed awareness the reality of our post-*Shoah* and post-Auschwitz lives by recreating such life-cycle ceremonies as do honor and respect to the Jewish religious tradition while likewise addressing the reality of our own history. To ignore either is to do violence to both.

Birthing and family events begin the life cycle all over again, and the comments made thus far with regard to birth, growth, maturation, and their attendant rituals and ceremonies before and after the *Shoah* remain equally applicable. *Hanukkat ha-Bayit*, the dedication of the family's-couple's-individual's new home is likewise cause for celebration.

Orthodox ritual is nonexistent, although the "owner" is expected to recite four Psalms, 15, 101, 121, and 30 (pp. 55-59); Conservative ritual substitutes the saying of Psalms 128, 101, and 127 together with Proverbs 24:3-4. *Devarim* (Deuteronomy) 6:4-9 is contained within the part of the dedication ceremony wherein the *mezuzah* is affixed to the doorpost with the commanded blessing, "Praised are You, O Lord our God, King of the universe, who sanctified us with Your commandments and commanded us to affix the *mezuzah* to the doorposts of our homes." Additional prayers frame the ritual (pp. 59-64).

The Reform *Rabbi's Manual* dedication has blessings over bread, wine, and Bible, referred to as "the Law by which Israel has ever lived," framed by other prayers. Turning to the *mezuzah*, reference is made to "our need to love Him and to obey His Law." The blessing for the affixing of the *mezuzah* itself is a "commanded blessing" (pp. 50-53). *Ma'agele Tsedek* does not even include any dedication ceremony or ritual whatsoever.

Again, as before, the *Shoah* is ignored and the implications denied. Here, too, there is room for creative liturgical expression taking into consideration everything thus far written.

No "conversion ritual" whatsoever appears in the Orthodox *Hamadrikh*. After a lengthy Introduction-explanation (pp. 67-69), the Conservative ritual begins with "commanded blessings" for circumcision-ritual recircumcision (not translated!) and ritual immersion with the passage from *Yehezkel* (Ezekiel) 36:25-28. Then follows a rabbinic prayer, *Devarim* (Deuteronomy) 6:4-9, *Ruth* 1:16-17, rabbinic address, reading of Certificate of Acceptance into the Jewish Faith (two choices given), and additional prayers (pp. 70-81).

The Reform *Rabbi's Manual* begins with welcoming blessings, asks a series of five questions of the candidate for conversion, recites *Devarim* (Deuteronomy) 6:4-9 and *Ruth* 1:16-17, additional prayers, provides for the public declaration of the Hebrew name chosen, and ends with a rabbinic blessing. Provision is likewise made for the public reading of the Certificate of Conversion (pp. 17-22).

Ma'agele Tsedek provides for a rather lengthy ceremony (pp. 199-217) composed of various parts: welcoming blessings, the asking of *six* rather than five questions, affirmation by candidate with opportunities for his or her reading participation, *Ruth* 1:16-17, and the reading of the Certificate. Additional ceremonies are included for ritual immersion, circumcision-ritual recircumcision, both of which include commanded obligatory blessings, and infant or child ritual immersion. Public prayers conclude.

To "convert" to Judaism and take one's place with the Jewish people *after* the *Shoah* in a world offering no guarantees that such horrors will not once again afflict the Jewish people is an act of tremendous courage and truly deserves to be publicly acknowledged as such. In a world that saw the destruction of 6 million Jews, 1.5 million of whom were under the age of 18 and 1 million of those under the age of 12, such a ceremony and ritual *must* give voice to the positive life-affirming statement made by one not born into the Jewish people but who consciously and sincerely chooses to identify with the Jewish people and Jewish way of life. Perhaps, with the possible exception of the birthing rituals, the conversion rituals most poignantly force us to confront the *Shoah* will all of its philosophic and religio-theological implications. To simply ignore the *Shoah* in the life of one who now chooses to become one with the Jewish people is an injustice to the individual, the event itself, and the sacred memories of those who are no more. *All* such ceremonies now need to be either modified or re-created with full knowledge of what it means to choose such a path in the aftermath of Auschwitz.

Decay: Aging and Sickness, Death of Parents, and Divorce

None of the three major Jewish religious movements, Orthodox, Conservative, or Reform, contains within its rabbinic manuals any prayers whatsoever that address aging; again, a missed opportunity. All three, however, do address the health of those who are ill or about to undergo surgery or those who have successfully recovered. All three address God directly in appeals for the well-being of the afflicted, collectively understanding God to (1) hear and respond to earnest and sincere prayers and petitions, and (2) interact positively with the human community for its own betterment (Orthodox, pp. 99-104; Conservative, pp. 84-94; Reform I, pp. 55-58; Reform II, pp. 191-197). Juxtaposed to the *Shoah*, however, both notions are terribly problematic, to say the very, very least: God hears and responds to individual and collective appeals for return to health, but neither hears nor responds when the anguished petitions of the victims of the *Shoah* are left unanswered? God interacts positively with His or Her human children when what is at stake is illness, but *not* when the disease is early, atrocious death at the hands of other human beings?

The tragic reality of the *Shoah* is that this understanding of God and God's relationship to our world is either horribly naive, based upon wishful thinking, or terribly inaccurate, misreading both Jewish religious tradition and the actualities of Jewish and world history. Although I would prefer to opt for naivete and wishful thinking, if truth now be told, the one leads to the other: *Out of our strong desire to interact with a God who continues to take care of us, we deny the evidence of experience most awfully when that evidence contradicts our desires and beliefs.* God has shown us over and over again His or Her inability to respond directly or indirectly to our prayers and requests, including the *Shoah*; to continue to offer them up is only to compound the felony, suspend what we know to be truth and reality, and increase our frustration out of our seeming refusal to confront the abyss directly and emerge the stronger for having done so.

Better to give voice and verbalization to our own inner resources with which to combat illness and disease—family love, sense of humor, better care and knowledge of our bodies, diet, and exercise, medical skill and knowledge—than to fruitless appeals to a God incapable of answering or unwilling to do so. Consistent with the emphasis of Chapter 3, "The Crises of Prayer," such verbalization would take the form of thanksgiving for life itself, however long or short the journey, and meaningful covenants of dialogue with all those involved with the one who is ill. Strength to "fight off" illness and disease is thus derived from both and from the prayerful words of the Jewish religious tradition now rewritten and reinterpreted with this understanding and not ignoring the reality of the *Shoah* and a God who was not there.

(The death of parents is addressed in the next section dealing with funeral, grief, and bereavement practices.)

Only the newer Reform rabbi's manual *Ma'agele Tsedek* includes a "ritual of release" ceremony (pp. 97-102) in the sad eventuality of divorce, as well as a copy of the "document of separation" (pp. 103-104). Both are designed to ease and soften the pain of divorce and regain whatever is left of mutual respect and trust, ideally diminishing hostility in the process. Concern for the children is likewise expressed. Reference is made to Babylonian Talmud *Gittin* 90b, "even the altar sheds tears," and *Divrei Hayamim Alef* (I Chronicles) 12:19, the end of which verse reads "truly God is your Helper."

The aforementioned Document of Separation, as well as the traditional form of both the Orthodox and Conservative *Get* (Bill of Divorcement) do not raise theological problems of any consequence with regard to the *Shoah* and the issues raised in this book. Divorce itself, like the death of loved ones, is traumatic enough, and the sensitivities to which I have already alluded are sufficient enough and need no elaboration. And, although some may be critical of the traditional community's "giving of the *Get*" to the woman as demeaning, and the male bias of traditional Judaism as equally demeaning, discussion of these particular concerns falls outside the purview of this volume.

Death: Confession and Dying, Funeral and Yahrtzeit

Prayers of *Vidui* (Confession) are found in all four rabbis' manuals: Orthodox (pp. 105-106); Conservative (pp. 96-98); Reform I (pp. 59-61); Reform II (pp. 106-109). All direct their "voices" to God, asking forgiveness of whatever sins have been committed during the life's journey, and from present suffering. Death itself is thus understood by all to be the final act of atonement and contrition. The theological position is universally that of the historical-traditional one of a God who acknowledges our very presence, interacts with us, and responds accordingly. No alternative possibilities are suggested even though death is imposed and is inescapable. Nor is the reality of the *Shoah* anywhere in evidence, representing as it does a direct contradiction to this theology: *The wanton, murderous deaths of Six Million innocent Jews at the hands of their own species was in no way, manner, shape, or form an atoning for any sins whatsoever, real or imagined.* Although some may have been able to offer *vidui* prior to their murder and slaughter, the overwhelming majority of those slain did not nor should they have done so. And although "confession may be good for the 'soul'," in the aftermath of the *Shoah*, acknowledgment of the errors of one's ways during the life's journey may have real psychological benefit prior to death, the appropriate audience is now one's own family and friends and community with whom one *should* make peace, but not necessarily God, whose

own seeming impotence during the *Shoah* invalidates the Divine as
the worthy recipient of such *vidui.*

In the evolution of an almost 2,000-year-old religious tradition,
practices, customs, and traditions surrounding the funeral are legion.
To be sure, the function of the funeral service itself is twofold: (1) to
give comfort to the survivors, and (2) to give honor and respect to the
deceased. The Orthodox service (pp. 124-136) acknowledges the
presence of God as the Author and Giver and Remover of Life, the
very transitoriness of life itself, includes *Tehillim* (Psalms) 123, 16, 49,
16, 91, as well as other "appropriate" prayers stressing all these
themes. The Conservative service (pp. 101-133) follows this general
idea and includes readings from *Yishayahu* (Isaiah) 40:6-8, 41:10;
Tehillim (Psalms) 103:13-17, 73:26, 24:1-6, 15, 23, 90, 91; *Malachi*
2:6; *Mishlei* (Proverbs) 31; *Shmuel Bet* (II Samuel) 12, 19:1; *Iyov*
(Job) 28:1-2, 12; *Yirmiyahu* (Jeremiah) 8:18, 23; Babylonian Talmud
Berachot 17a; *Wisdom of Solomon, Ben Sira* 30:3-5; and additional
prayers. The Reform *Rabbi's Manual* offers three different funeral
services (pp. 63-90), again following the previous understanding, and
includes readings from *Tehillim* (Psalms) 121, 90, 23, 16; *Wisdom
of Solomon* 3, and additional prayers. *Ma'agele Tsedek* in its own
service (pp. 111-162) includes readings from *Tehillim* (Psalms) 16, 1,
15, 23, 90, 121; *Kohelet* (Ecclesiastes) 3; *Mishlei* 31; *Yishayahu*
(Isaiah) 40:6-8, and additional prayers. All the manuals include *Ale
Malei Rachamim* ("O God, Full of Compassion") and *Kaddish,*
("Magnified and sanctified by Thy Name, O God").

As is the case with the *vidui*, the theological understanding of
God is one who cares, is concerned, and is actively involved with
His or Her human children. Nothing in any of these services gives
voice to the reality of the *Shoah* nor any other ways of understanding
the "Divine-human encounter."

Two additional "events" surrounding death are contained in all
four rabbis' manuals: dedication of a tombstone, and consecration of
a cemetery (Orthodox, pp. 156-163 and 164-177; Conservative,
pp. 137-145 and 148-154; Reform I, pp. 93-99 and 100-103; Reform II,
pp. 165-179 and 180-189). All include various Torah-Scripture verses,
primarily from *Sefer Tehillim* (Book of Psalms), various additional
prayers appropriate, in the first instance to the deceased (i.e., male,
female, underage child), and *Kaddish Y'tom* (mourner's memorial
prayer). Requests are made of God, again in the first instance, to
"soften the pain of loss," and praising God for the life of the deceased
while recognizing its brevity. In the instance of the dedication of a
cemetery, God is recognized as the Author of Life, given praise and

thanks, and requested to take care of both the deceased and the living.

Again, as has so often been the case with *all* of these life-cycle events, the understanding of God is that of the historically traditional one of an interactive Deity concerned with and interactive with His Jewish children and the rest of the human community. As an event of cataclysmic proportions, however, the *Shoah*, is not addressed in any appreciable form for the generation who continues to confront the loss of Six Million Innocents and the religious and theological implications of the absence of God during the years 1933(39)-1945. The need to rethink and rewrite those additional prayers after the *Shoah* is self-evident. Other Torah-Scripture verses and passages need to be included that refocus these ceremonies and rituals on the human being and human community rather than on God.

What has been suggested in this chapter has been the conscious need to *rethink* the rationale for all Jewish life-cycle events, supplying new understandings where necessary, modifying others where appropriate, and disregarding entirely both events and understandings where warranted. For those Jews who wish to continue their positive affirmations of their Jewish selves and their involvement in Jewish religious doing after the *Shoah*, it *is* now possible to do so without sacrificing either personal integrity, religious sensitivity or historical knowledge. I leave to the creative liturgists of our Jewish world the poetic responsibilities now entailed in the rewriting of these life-cycle events consistent with all of the concerns voiced thus far, turning now to the holiday-festival calendar and an examination of the historically supplied reasons for their doing. Again, the caveat is the same as that applied to the life cycle: The specific manner of observance of this or that Jewish holiday may not necessarily change upon examination in light of the *Shoah*, but its rationale now needs to be rethought to see if its justification any longer makes sense. The courage to do so and to posit new ideas, modify old ones, and preserve those worthy of preservation is consistent, I do fully believe, with the integrity of the Jewish religious tradition as it has historically evolved over the centuries, always taking into consideration the world events of which we both are a part and a recipient.

Notes

1. To date, the Reconstructionists have not yet published their own; its colleagues either borrow from the other three movements or create their own expressions.

2. Hyman E. Goldin, *Hamadrikh: The Rabbi's Guide: A Manual of Jewish Rituals, Ceremonials and Customs,* revised ed. (New York: Hebrew Publishing Company, 1956). Jules Harlow, ed., *Likutei Tephillah: A Rabbi's Manual* (New York: The Rabbinical Assembly, 1965). *Rabbi's Manual,* revised ed. (New York: Central Conference of American Rabbis, 1961). David Polish, ed., *Ma'agele Tsedek: Rabbi's Manual* (New York: Central Conference of American Rabbis, 1988).

3. The Reform Movement's commitment to the equality of all predates the *Shoah.*

4. "Hearken Israel! Adonai is our God, Adonai alone! Praised be His Name whose glorious kingdom is forever and ever," following *Devarim* (Deuteronomy) 6:4.

5. I have only recently heard of one Reform congregation in the Midwest where the rabbi prefers the term *Ben Torah* or *Bat Torah,* "son" or "daughter of Torah" to describe this coming of age ceremony. Although certainly addressing the difficulty of the notion of *Mitzvah,* this labeling, to my way of thinking is, also, problematic on two levels: (1) It does not start from the perspective of the reality of the *Shoah,* and (2) it does not address the equally difficult question of one's relation to Scripture itself post-Auschwitz.

6. No slight whatsoever is here intended to the "middle-born" whose departure may very well be equally difficult.

6

Rethinking the Jewish Festival Cycle: The Calendar in Question

Celebration and commemoration of the festival cycle, like the life cycle in the previous chapter, will also have to be rethought since the *Shoah*. No longer does it make sense to continue to celebrate or sanctify this or that festival for the historically traditional reasons previously given in Jewish or Christian religious traditions. Again, though the practices themselves may not vary in the slightest from the ways in which the Jewish people presently practice their celebration of these events, or have done so in the past, the *rationale* behind their celebration now demands new understandings of these events in the post-*Shoah* world. No more can *Pesach* (Passover), for example, be viewed as God's liberation of the Jewish people from slavery and bondage in Egypt when the slavery and bondage of Nazi Germany resulted in the deaths and degradations of so many. "Why one and not the other?" continues to be the question. The central core issue remains not one of practice and commitment, but the "whys" of those practices and the "wherefores" of those commitments since the *Shoah*.

For the purpose of this chapter, we may group our Jewish holidays, holy days, festivals, and fast days in the following four categories:

1. *Biblical—Major* (that is, those days that derive their origins from the first Five Books of Moses): *Shabbat* (Sabbath), *Pesach* (Passover), *Sefirat ha-Omer* (Counting of the Omer), *Shavuot* (Weeks), *Rosh ha-Shanah* (New Year), *Yom Kippur* (Day of Atonement), *Sukkot* (Feast of Booths), *Shemini Atzeret* (Eighth Day of Solemn Assembly), and *Rosh Hodesh* (New Moon).
2. *Biblical—Minor* (that is, those days that derive their origins from the Torah outside of the first Five Books of Moses): *Hanukkah* (Festival of Dedication) and *Purim* (Festival of Esther).

3. *Rabbinic* (that is, those days that derive their origins beyond the
    time of the Torah text): *Lag B'Omer* (33rd Day of the Omer),
    Tisha B'Av (9th Day of Av; Collective Day of Mourning), *Simchat
    Torah* (Celebration of the Torah), and *Tu b'Shevat* (15th Day of
    Shevat; Jewish Arbor Day).
4. *Contemporary* (that is, those days that derive their origins from
    our modern period): *Yom ha-Shoah* (*Shoah* Remembrance Day)
    and *Yom ha-Atzmaut* (Israeli Independence Day).

Biblical—Major

Shabbat

The fourth of the so-called Ten Commandments (*Aseret ha-
Dibrot*, better Ten Essential Statements) appearing in *Sefer Shemot*
(Book of Exodus), Chapter 20, reads as follows:

> [8] Remember the sabbath day and keep it holy. [9] Six days
> you shall labor and do all your work, [10] but the seventh day is
> a sabbath of the Lord your God; you shall not do any work—
> you, your son or daughter, your male or female slave, or your
> cattle, or the stranger who is within your settlements. [11] For in
> six days the Lord made heaven and earth and sea, and all that is
> in them, and He rested on the seventh day; therefore the Lord
> blessed the sabbath day and hallowed it.

The deuteronomic restatement in *Sefer Devarim*, Chapter 5, is,
in some ways, an expanded text:

> [12] Observe the seventh day and keep it holy, as the Lord your
> God has commanded you. [13] Six days you shall labor and do all
> your work, [14] but the seventh day is a sabbath of the Lord
> your God: you shall not do any work—you, your son or daughter,
> your male or female slave, your ox or your ass, or any of your
> cattle, or the stranger in your settlements, so that your male and
> female slave may rest as you do. [15] Remember that you were a
> slave in the land of Egypt and the Lord your God freed you from
> there with a mighty hand and an outstretched arm; therefore
> the Lord your God has commanded you to observe the sabbath
> day.

Two of the most popular *Shabbat* hymns are the *V'shamru* and
the *Yism'chu*. Their translations are as follows:

V'shamru

The people of Israel shall keep the Sabbath, observing the Sabbath in every generation as a covenant for all time. It is a sign for ever between Me and the people of Israel, for in six days the Eternal God made heaven and earth, and on the seventh day He rested from His labors. (*Gates of Prayer*, p. 133)

Yism'chu

Those who keep the Sabbath and call it a delight shall rejoice in Your kingdom. All who hallow the seventh day shall be gladdened by Your goodness. This day is Israel's festival of the spirit, sanctified and blessed by You, the most precious of days, a symbol of the joy of creation. (*Gates of Prayer*, p. 154)

Therefore, the dominating themes of the Sabbath according to an historically traditional Jewish and Christian understanding are already self-evident in the biblical texts and rabbinic additions. Observance of the Sabbath is (1) cessation from productive work in emulation of a Creator Deity who "rested" and commanded such imitation, and (2) a primary means of joyously sanctifying ("making holy," separate, apart) the unique covenantal relationship between God and the Jewish people. For the Rabbis who expanded the concept of "work" to include thirty-nine archetypal categories,[1] the Sabbath was, in addition, a foretaste of the advent of the Messiah and the equivalent of all other Torahitic precepts.[2]

Quite obviously, after the *Shoah*, the one concept of Sabbath worship that retains its validity is that of emulation of the Creator God who worked and rested. Neither being commanded to do so nor signifying the covenant between God and the Jewish people retains its legitimacy in light of what has previously been written about these topics given the *Shoah*'s reality. Also, the *Siddur* (Sabbath and festival prayer book) and *Machzor* (High Holy Day prayer book) prayers will have to be rethought and rewritten, if not in the original Hebrew on the part of those who would wish to retain the historically traditional language of the sacred, though a Hebrew rewrite is cetainly equally appropriate, then, at the very least, in their translation, to be more honestly reflective of Jewish life in a post-Auschwitz world. The stringent interpretations of Sabbath practices as observed in the Orthodox communities and to a lesser extent in non-Orthodox communities regarding what one may or may not do on the Sabbath is now open to reinterpretation: To be sure, celebration of the day, beginning and ending religiously with prayer and study, celebration of family togetherness with family-related activities and meals, refraining from gainful employment in which one is engaged the other five or six days are all values to be further emphasized and stressed after the *Shoah*. Jews who now wish to be religious Jews, survivors, their children and others, *must* be accorded the freedom and respect to develop their own meaningful Sabbath equilibrium.

Pesach

As is so well known, the celebration of the Passover is the celebration of the liberation of the ancient Jewish people *by God* from the slavery of the hell of Egyptian bondage into the freedom of the Promised Land of Israel with an intermittent forty-year sojourn and wandering in the deserts of Sinai during which time God and the Jewish people entered into covenant. Indeed, "according to tradition, the Passover rites were divinely ordained as a permanent reminder of God's deliverance of His people from Egyptian bondage."[3] The details of both the slave experience and the liberation experience are set forth in *Sefer Shemot* (Book of Exodus). The rabbinic evolution of the now home-based ritual celebration as contained in the special prayer book known as the *Haggadah* ("The Story") involves a retelling of the story itself with appropriate prayers of thanksgiving to God who liberated the Jewish people.

After the *Shoah*, it is no longer religiously creditable to speak of God's liberation of the Jewish people from Egypt but not from Germany or Poland or Russia or France. It is no longer morally creditable to give thanks for one liberation, that of Egypt, but not for the other, that of Nazi-terrorized Europe. Better to focus on the liberation event itself: that the Jewish people realized it could not pursue its own religious journey in slavery and *consciously chose* escape from Egypt as the only viable means toward religious self-fulfillment, having been denied such an opportunity under Pharaonic leadership. The *Haggadah* itself may very well have to be rewritten, honestly downplaying God's *active* role in the process and, instead, further emphasizing God as a *source* of inspiration for such liberation. In light of Chapter 3, "The Crises of Prayer," certain prayers themselves may likewise have to be rethought and rewritten.

Entering into a covenant at Sinai during this time is equally if not more problematic and can no longer be seen or understood as part and parcel of the historical Passover experience. Better now to emphasize a call to "covenants of dialogue" after Passover. (Having already discussed my idea of covenant in Chapter 2, "Covenant: Involuntary? Voluntary? Nonexistent?" little else needs now be written on that topic.[4])

Sefirat Ha-Omer

Based on *Vayikra* (Leviticus) 23:9 and following, the first sheaf of the harvest was to be brought to the *cohain* (priest) who in turn waved it as an offering to God, symbolic of yet another successful agricultural season, in the process granting permission to eat the fruits of the harvest. To be sure, the symbolic ritual was a thanksgiving ritual performed before God without whom the harvest itself would not have been successful. One was then required to "count seven weeks" (49 days, the "Omer season"), after which the festival of *Shavuot* (Festival of Weeks) was celebrated. Biblically, the sheaf, primarily and later exclusively of barley, was brought to the Temple; rabbinically, only the formulaic "Today is the first day of the *Omer*. . . . Today is the eighth day of the *Omer*, making one day and one week of the *Omer*," and so forth, continues to be recited in the *Ma'ariv* or evening service. Sometime during the talmudic period, the "counting of the *Omer*" assumed a much more solemn character than originally intended, with no weddings to be performed.[5]

Acknowledging God as *Borei Olam*, Creator of the World, Creator of a world of possibilities, as spelled out in Chapter 1, "The Problem with God," is not inconsistent with the "counting of the *Omer*" after the *Shoah*. Letting it serve as a symbolic "bridge" between the festivals of *Pesach* and *Shavuot*, keeping these two major holidays ever present in the minds of the Jewish people is equally not inconsistent. However, the logic of solemnity surrounding this period, specifically forbidding marriages, is no longer either viable or meaningful in light of the *Shoah*; better to look for those opportunities and occasions in which marriages are encouraged for a community horrifically devastated by the tragedy of the *Shoah*. Also, *directly* attributing economic success to God, agricultural success no longer being reality for the overwhelming majority of the world's Jews, no longer makes sense. Better this initial acknowledging of God as the Creator of that world wherein by virtue of one's talents, abilities, and skills success becomes real than any causal link whatsoever. As previously stated, certain prayers surrounding the *Omer* may have to be rethought and rephrased, though not the counting formula itself.

Shavuot

Signaling the beginning of the *wheat* rather than the barley harvest, Torahitically, *Shavuot* is known by three names: the "Feast of Weeks," the "Feast of the Harvest," and the "day of the First Fruits."

Rabbinically, following *Shemot* (Exodus) 19, the festival of *Shavuot* was transformed into *zeman mattan Torahteinu* ("the time of the giving of the Torah"); that is, "the anniversary of the giving of the Torah at Sinai."[6] Contemporary non-Orthodox Jewish movements celebrate and associate "Confirmation" with this holiday.

Again, following the *Omer* period, little is in conflict in, again, celebrating economic success, individually and collectively, in a world where a Creator God could initiate such possibilities, dependent, however, on human initiative. Extremely problematic, however, is the latter rabbinic notion of God *giving* the Scriptures to the Jewish People at Sinai after the fact and reality of the *Shoah*. Whatever else may be said of this text, it should be both obvious and readily apparent that the Scriptures, like everything else in Jewish life, historically, contemporarily, futuristically, is *not* predicated on an interactive Deity who gave, gives, will give anything to the Jewish people, or anyone else for that matter. Scriptures and all else in Jewish life are the changing, evolutionary responses of the Jewish people to its ongoing perception of the Divine-human encounter-relationship or lack thereof, always taking into consideration the historical realities of the times in which we are living.[7] Prayers for *Shavuot* that suggest otherwise must, of course, be rewritten and rethought.

Rosh ha-Shanah

Referred to in the Torah as the day of the blowing of the *shofar* (ram's horn) and occurring at the start of the *seventh* month, better known by its Babylonian name *Tishri*, scholarly conclusion is that *Rosh ha-Shanah* may very well have signaled the start of the economic-agricultural year. Ultimately and rabbinically, however, it was to replace *Nisan* as the first month of the calendar year, when, according to the Rabbis, humanity stands before its Sovereign God in judgment as to the merits of its deeds during the past year (i.e., who will live and who will die during the course of the year to come), and start of a ten-day penitential season. Additionally, the Rabbis concluded, *Rosh ha-Shanah* was in fact the very day on which the world itself was physically created by God.

After the Shoah, *it is not now Jewish humanity that stands in judgment before God, but God who now stands in judgment before humanity and humanity that now stands in judgment before itself.* To, again, affirm an historically traditional understanding of God as Punisher and Rewarder after Auschwitz is now to mock the deaths of so many innocent victims and to raise anew the haunting question, "What sin[s] had the Jewish People committed, men, women, and children, which merited the *Shoah*?" Because there is no convincing answer to this question, better to remove discussion, reference, and prayers to God as Judge, and focus, instead, on acknowledging the "dark side of humanity [and the noninvolvement of the Divine]," condemning to the point of expressing outrage at those who were active participants, expressing profound sadness at those who were bystanders, and expressing solidarity with those who were victims and rescuers. Independent of *Yom ha-Shoah* discussed later, *Rosh ha-Shanah* is an appropriate annual stock taking of the very worst of which humanity is capable and a vowing never to be guilty of such repetition again, along with acknowledgment of the very best of which other humans showed themselves capable and a commitment of oneself to emulate such extraordinarily courageous and loving behavior.

The secondary theme of the "birthday" of the creation of the world, as has already been expressed, is not in conflict with either the *Shoah* or my understanding of God as *Borei Olam*. Celebrating the creation of the world, of its possibilities and its potential after the *Shoah,* is now an affirmation of the triumph of life over death, and much more important and suggestive than perhaps heretofore realized. Renewed emphasis on this theme is, therefore, to be encouraged and expanded.

Yom Kippur

Concluding the ten-day penitential season begun with *Rosh ha-Shanah*, the essence of this "Day of Atonement" is found in the Torah verse *Vayikra* (Leviticus) 16:30: "For on this day shall atonement be made for you, to cleanse you; from all your sins shall ye be clean before the Lord." No manner of work was to be conducted on this day, and special offerings were to be brought to the Temple in Jerusalem. In the Second Temple period, the High Priest, dressed in white, after a period of purification and sexual abstinence, entered the "Holy of Holies" and there pronounced the Four Letter Name of God, the Tetragrammaton,[8] symbolically taking upon himself punishment for the sins committed by collective Israel and beseeching God's forgiveness. Rabbinically, it has evolved into an all-day fast with worship services conducted throughout the day.

Recognition and condemnation for the sins of active involvement and participation in the *Shoah* and apathy and indifference to the *Shoah* are certainly appropriate to this *Yom Kippur*, as they are to *Rosh ha-Shanah*. At its conclusion, however, what must dominate thinking is the vow never to allow its repetition and not to stand idly by and allow others their participation in such horrific genocidal-like events. Because those who were biologically old enough to have participated in or experienced the events of the *Shoah* will all-too-soon pass from the scene, *personal* guilt and shame for those of us born after these events should not enter into these thoughts, though honesty in reflecting how we would have behaved under those circumstances (or might yet act under anything comparable) is called for. Again, recognition, condemnation, sadness, and memorial are all appropriate, and the liturgies of the day must reflect these perspectives as well as the vows of commitment. Thus, this shift in emphasis for *Yom Kippur* after the *Shoah* will no longer be on the sins committed yesterday but on the firm resolution to sin no more. Prayers appropriate to this newer understanding will have to be rewritten or possibly created.

Sukkot

The third of the *Sh'losh Regalim* or "pilgrimage festivals" to Jerusalem, after *Pesach* and *Shavuot*, this "Feast of Booths" or "Tabernacles," coming five days after *Yom Kippur* and celebrated for seven days, commemorates both the temporary dwelling-places of the Israelites during the forty years of wandering in the desert and the end of the harvest season in ancient Israel. Reminders of both continue in rabbinic tradition with the obligation to erect such *sukkot* (booths) temporarily for seven (now eight) days, dwelling in them if possible or at least eating one's family meals therein, and the display of the *arba minim* (four agricultural species of palm, willow, myrtle, and citron).

Like *Pesach* and *Shavuot*, as suggested previously, celebration of both Israel's liberation experience, downplaying the questionable role of God, and Israel's agricultural beginnings do not conflict with the *Shoah*. Prayers and other ritual expressions that reflect this understanding likewise do not represent or pose problems for the committed religious Jew after the *Shoah* who wishes to affirm both his or her Jewish self and Jewish identity. It is only that historically traditional notion as understood by the majority of the world's Jews that continues to attribute all success to God's active intervention and continuing involvement, despite and after the *Shoah*, that poses difficulties to and for a rethought and reformulated Jewish faith.

Shemini Atzeret

Concluding the Festival of *Sukkot*, this "Eighth Day of Solemn Assembly" is found in *Bamidbar* (Numbers) 29:35 and is, like the others, a day on which no meaningful or gainful work was to take place. A post-Auschwitz understanding of its observance is, therefore, to be included in that of *Sukkot* itself as well as *Simchat Torah* discussed later.

Rosh Hodesh

The appearance of each new moon on the Hebrew calendar in ancient Israel was cause for celebration with the bringing of an additional (*Musaf*) sacrifice to the Temple, following *Bamidbar* (Numbers) 28:11-15. Rabbinically, on the Sabbath preceding, announcement and prayer is made in the synagogue, asking God's blessing for the month ahead.

As has already been mentioned, celebration of new beginnings in the life of the resurrected Jewish people after Auschwitz is to be welcomed, perhaps more so than ever before. Prayers and rituals that now honor yet another month of life, health, peace, prosperity, and joy are certainly to be celebrated. Seeing in *Rosh Hodesh* additional possibilities for thanksgiving in Jewish religious life may go far beyond what biblically and rabbinically had been the case and return us to an even earlier biblical understanding. But, given contemporary history and experience, here may very well be a profound illustration of the adaptive and sustaining power of the Jewish religious faith, heritage, and tradition in ways not originally intended.

Biblical—Minor

Hanukkah

Celebrating the victory over the Syrio-Greeks in the year 162 B.C.E. after a protracted three-year struggle, as well as the rededication of the Temple sanctuary in Jerusalem by the Hasmonean followers of Judah ha-Maccabee, this eight-day festival detailed in the *Sifre Maccabee* (Books of Maccabees I and II) is among the most popular of all Jewish festivals and holidays and enjoyed by children of all ages. Known as either the "Feast of Dedication" or the "Festival of Lights," the tradition of lighting the *menorah* (candelabrum) arose in early rabbinic times. Gift giving and special foods associated with the festival are an especially important part of its celebration.

Commemorating past victories over those who would oppress and do worse to the Jewish people represents no conflict with the *Shoah*. Rededication and reconsecrating the ancient Temple likewise represents no conflict. Attributing both military success and religious renewal to Divine intervention in light of the *Shoah* remains an ongoing difficulty. Better to focus on these events as part of our collective history celebrating our own commitments and exercise of talents, skills, and energies than God's active role in them.

Additionally, *Hanukkah* in its dedication and re-dedication of the Temple sanctuary now presents us with an additional opportunity for the renewal of our religious commitments after the *Shoah* not yet addressed by the Jewish religious tradition or by any of its denominations: Orthodox, Conservative, Reform, Reconstructionist. Recognizing fully and totally the religious, theological, and philosophical implications of the *Shoah*, what may very well be appropriate at the celebration of *Hanukkah* is the annual celebration of personal, family, and community religious commitments; a renewal of "vows" of religious affirmation, despite the difficulties of doing so in a post-Auschwitz world. Such a "statement of intent" might be the following:

> We want to be religiously sensitive and religiously mature Jews in this world after the *Shoah*, drawing upon the resources of our Jewish past and our Jewish present to do so. May we, therefore, use this occasion of *Hanukkah* to further commit ourselves to our goals and objectives, never ceasing to ask questions and always questioning our answers. May we, out of our struggling and out of our wrestling, come to find that inner peace and contentment after the *Shoah* for which we continue to search, letting our quest renew in us the strength and energy to go forward.

Purim

According to *Megillat Esther* (Scroll or Book of Esther) 9:20-28, *Purim* is "the feast instituted . . . by Mordecai to celebrate the deliverance of the Jews from Haman's plot to kill them."[9] Its carnivallike aspect, replete with costume parade and parody, continues to make it a popular Jewish festival, despite the historical difficulties in identifying the events described therein as well as the major characters portrayed. Ironically, the miraculous salvation of the Jews from this attempted annihilation is attributed in the rabbinic tradition to God, though God is *never* mentioned in the text of the *Megillah* (but *is* mentioned in the Greek translation). *Thus, though certainly never realized in its applicability to the Shoah, historical precedent now exists to celebrate Jewish self-realization and self-actualization with-*

out the historically traditional reference to Divine intervention and active involvement. Additionally, by an expansion of its liturgical and ritual possibilities, *Purim* may be seen as a "metaphor" for all of the unsuccessful past attempts to destroy the Jewish people. From Haman to Hitler, there have always been those who, for whatever reason, have sought to exterminate the Jewish people. Our continuing existence on this planet is both tribute and testimony to our strength, vitality, and determination in the ongoing face of adversity. *Purim*, too, after the *Shoah*, thus has the potential for our Jewish people to expand its original intention and reinvolve us in a meaningful religious journey, though perhaps not one for which it was originally created.

Rabbinic

Lag b'Omer

This thirty-third day of the counting of the *Omer* during the period between *Pesach* and *Shavuot*, known as the "Scholar's Holiday," celebrates, according to rabbinic tradition, the end of a plague that devastated the Jewish community of Palestine during the Roman oppression. It also became the anniversary of the death of Rabbi Simeon bar Yochai, one of the leaders of that community, in Meron, who asked that it not be observed with mourning but with singing and dance. *Lag b'Omer* thus became something of a celebratory day during this rather solemn period and evolved into one day during this seven-week period when weddings could be performed.

As has already been stated, both recognition of historical events in the life of the Jewish people and celebratory occasions subsequent to the *Shoah* pose no conflict. If anything, we should increasingly look for more and more ways to celebrate and affirm life after the *Shoah*. Only attributing the cessation of the aforementioned plague to God's intervention would present a theological problem resolved, according to this author, now in a way strictly at variance with an historically traditional understanding but in accord with the reality of the years 1993(39)-1945.

Tisha b'Av

The ninth day of the Hebrew month of *Av* was set aside by the Rabbis of the Jewish religious tradition as "the traditional day of mourning for the destruction of the temples in Jerusalem" (in 586 B.C.E. and again in 70 C.E.).[10] As the Jewish people continued its historic journey, four additional events began to be associated with this day of mourning: (1) a decree was rendered forbidding the Israelites to enter the Promised Land after the Exodus on this day; (2) the last stronghold of the Bar Kochba revolt in 135 C.E. was destroyed on this day; (3) a heathen temple was established by the Romans in Jerusalem (renamed *Aelia Capitolina*) in 136 C.E. on this day; and (4) the expulsion from Spain in August of 1492 began on this day. Therefore,

> The ninth of Av thus became a symbol for all the persecutions and misfortunes of the Jewish people, for the loss of national independence and the sufferings in exile. The massacres of whole communities during the Crusades intensified this association.[11]

Therefore, personal mourning rites as well as synagogal mourning rites furthered the dark emphasis of this calendar day now assigned as recognition for *all* of the tragedies that have overtaken the House of Israel during the course of the centuries.

The logic of such a calendered day in the *religious* life of the Jewish people is beyond argument. The need both to remember and to mourn are equally important values for a historic people and a historical religious tradition. Subsequent to World War II, the debate in religious circles was whether or not the *Shoah* itself should now be included in such a listing. Traditional Orthodox communities, both in this country and abroad, opted for inclusion; nontraditional communities both here and abroad rejected this decision, seeing the *Shoah* as a unique, separate, and distinct event in Jewish life "worthy" of its own day of mourning, *Yom Ha-Shoah* (see later).

Because I, too, affirm the uniqueness and distinctiveness of the *Shoah*, in contrast to all other occasions of collective Jewish tragedy, I, too, see the obvious need for a separate occasion of mourning, theologically as well as historically.[12] And although I have no quarrel with the various practices that have evolved over the centuries in both Orthodox and non-Orthodox communities, personal as well as collective, I would only question any prayer that gives "thanks" to God for having spared those who survived and turns to God for future support, comfort, or strength.[13]

Simchat Torah

Celebrated at the end of the festival of *Sukkot*, this joyous day of dancing and parading marks the end of the Torah reading cycle and the beginning anew of the annual cycle of readings. Symbolically, celebrating both the end of the reading of *Devarim* (Deuteronomy) and the beginning of the reading of *Bereshit* (Genesis) further empha-sizes the treasure trove that is the Torah and that one *never* truly completes what one can learn from its study.

Quite obviously, the position taken throughout this book with regard to Torah is that of a nonliteralist-nonfundamentalist: Fraught with meaning, the words of Torah do not reflect either a 100 per-cent, totally accurate reporting of either events and conversations or the transmission of the very topics that they address. To say so, how-ever, does not in any way, manner, shape, or form demean either the sacred nature of the text or the values to be derived from its intensive study. As has been stated before: God did not give Moses the Torah at Sinai; the Torah is the evolving response of the Jewish people over the centuries to its changing perceptions of what it believes to be the Divine-human encounter or lack thereof. The Torah is, in fact, a compilation of oral traditions and ultimately of writings from various periods of time, with the earlier ones probably edited to some extent when set down in written form.

Now after the *Shoah*, *Simchat Torah* continues to be worthy of celebration. Torah continues to be a marvelous and centrally pre-cious resource for the life of the Jewish people, the accuracy of whose insights have not changed for thousands of years, though the interpretation of those insights continues to demand renewed reeval-uation as times and historical circumstances continue to change. Prayers and rituals that reflect this understanding post-*Shoah* are to be welcomed; prayers and rituals that do not are not.

Tu b'Shevat

This "New Year of the Trees" has special significance both in ancient and in contemporary Israel with its agricultural foci, and reminds us, again, of the importance of *trees* in human endeavors. One ancient tradition that celebrates *Tu b'Shevat* and that has con-temporary possibilities is the following: when a Jewish boy and girl were born, cedar and cypress trees were planted; when marriages took place, branches from each were used to fashion the *chuppah* (bridal canopy). Might such not also be possibilities within congre-gational families?

Also, with regard to the *Shoah*, might we not incorporate into our rethought and reconstituted liturgical expressions some mention of the importance trees held during World War II, hiding both sur-vivors and partisans in their fleeing and fighting the Nazis? Thus, the celebration of the importance of trees continues even in our own day and furthers meaning of this festival.

Contemporary

Yom ha-Shoah

Observed inside and outside of Israel since 1951, the Jewish people continue to look for and find increasingly meaningful ways both to mourn the loss of nearly 6 million of our brothers and sisters, parents and grandparents, sons and daughters, other family and friends, and to attempt to fathom both meaning and lessons from the *Shoah*. No standard manner of observance or practice has yet been formulated; communities and congregations continue to feel free to create for themselves those expressions that are uniquely their own. That the Jewish and Christian people *must* continue to do so is imperative and paramount and beyond discussion. Problems do, however, loom just over the horizon.

As those biologically connected to the events of the *Shoah* continue to pass from the scene, both witness and testimony will become things of the past, relegated to scholarly circles and videotaped efforts. Educating future generations about the *Shoah* likewise is becoming equally difficult. The challenge before us is to try and educate historically and religiously present and future generations of Jews and Christians that the *Shoah* is, indeed, a foundational event in both Western, Christian civilization, and Jewish history. Appropriate *religious* responses over time will change; what must not be allowed to change is its absence from the calendar of observance of congregations and communities.

As far as I am concerned, the only *inappropriate* or *inauthentic* part of any *Yom ha-Shoah* observance would be one that thanks God for having spared the Jewish people further tragedy and further reemphasizes the historically traditional understanding of God and God's relationship with the Jewish people. Were I to believe that such was indeed the case, there would have been little need to write this book. Obviously, I do not; and this book and its merits speak for themselves.

Yom ha-Atzmaut

Israel, the phoenix literally arising from the ashes of the *Shoah*, is now, in 1994, forty-six years old. Celebration of this primary expression of renewed life and commitment of the Jewish people after the horrendous tragedy of World War II is appropriate throughout the Jewish and non-Jewish world. In Israel itself,

it is marked by dancing in the streets, fireworks displays, picnic trips to the countryside, etc., as well as official ceremonies (e.g., the lighting of twelve torches for the Twelve Tribes of Israel) and organized open-air entertainments. . . . Independence Day is preceded by Remembrance Day (*Yom ha-Zikkaron*) for all those who have fallen in defense of Israel's independence and security.[14]

Cultural events and the awarding of various literary, music, and cultural prizes are also part of the celebration. Religious observances in Israel itself take a wide variety of expressions from creative efforts to special insertions in traditional services.

Outside of Israel, as is the case with *Yom ha-Shoah*, there is no standard manner of observance or practice in either congregations or Jewish and non-Jewish communities. Everything from fully constructed worship services to cultural, sports, and entertainment events to "civic celebrations" can thus far be found.

What Jews and non-Jews must guard against is the false theological equation that one of the *meanings* of the *Shoah* was that it was the necessary or sufficient precondition that allowed the State of Israel to come into being. This is both bad history and bad theology. Modern, that is eighteenth century and on, Zionists had been working diligently to bring about the re-creation of the Jewish State; true, the revelations of World War II opened more doors than were previously opened to them and made more people committed to settling in Israel or to others who wish to do so. Theologically, to say "Without the former (*Shoah*), there could not be the latter (Israel)," necessitates the theological refutation, "Better had there been no *Shoah* than for us to have an Israel today; the price paid was too great."

That the two are inextricably linked is true; one cannot celebrate the birth of the Third Jewish Commonwealth in our time without sadness that many of those who would have been there in celebration were callously and obscenely murdered before their time. All celebrations of *Yom ha-Atzmaut*, therefore, must taken into consideration and make reference to those members of the Jewish People, among whom were many committed Zionists, robbed of their opportunity to experience the "modern miracle of the Middle East." Not only those who fell in defense of Israel, but those who were exterminated without ever having had the chance to do so, are now included among those for whom it is appropriate to offer memorial prayers. Israel is, indeed, to be celebrated, but it is celebrated tinged with sadness, recognition that not all of the Jewish People who were there on May 5, 1948, were all those who should have been there. But we will continue to celebrate its rebirth nonetheless.

Having now presented both a rethought vision of both the life cycle and the holiday calendar of the Jewish people, it is appropriate that the last mentioned event is the newest: the celebration of *Yom ha-Atzmaut*, Israeli Independence Day. Now, after the *Shoah*, the question of a meaningful, relevant, and significant theological and religiously rethought understanding of the role of the State of Israel in the life of the Jewish people, and a religiously rethought understanding of the place of Zionism in Jewish theological thinking are paramount. It is to these questions that we turn in Chapter 7, "Israel and Zionism in Our Post-*Shoah* World."

Notes

1. See Babylonian Talmud, *Baba Kama* 2a for the complete listing.

2. Following a comment found in *Shemot Rabbah* 25:12.

3. *Encyclopedia Judaica* (Jerusalem: Keter Publishing House, 1971), vol. 13, P-Rec, #163.

4. Those who would argue for perceiving the Passover liberation experience as a *one-time* demonstration of Divine interaction and concern raise, to my way of thinking, all over again the "problems of God": Why one time and none else? Lack of caring and concern? Subsequent Divine impotence? Liberation from slavery and bondage but not from genocidal murder and obliteration? While, perhaps, attempting to remain faithful both to the textual tradition of the Torah and its subsequent rabbinic evolution, its does almost nothing to address the realities of the *Shoah*.

5. *Encyclopedia Judaica*, vol. 12, Min-O, #1382 ff.

6. *Encyclopedia Judaica*, vol. 14, Red-Si, #1319 ff.

7. Scriptures may, therefore, be very well understood as the creative human response to what was truly believed to be Divine inspiration or action. That there are now those among us, members of the Second Generation, who are now no longer comfortable with even this possibility is now obvious—but not necessarily in total conflict: To say that something is done in response to "Divine inspiration" or the perception of Divine inspiration is, in truth, to still admit an ignorance of the "ways of God." What is at issue, however, is God's *direct action or intervention* in the affairs of humanity rather than what lies behind them; and here, with regard to the *Shoah*, God is found wanting.

8. Yod, Hey, Vav, Hey.

9. *Encyclopedia Judaica*, vol. 13, P-Rec, #1389.

10. *Encyclopedia Judaica*, vol. 1, Anh-Az, #936.

11. Ibid.

12. The list cited previously does *not* address the radical difference in antisemitic response: from that of pogrom to that of total genocidal extermination and annihilation.

13. I do think Reform Judaism has erred, however, in removing commemoration of *Tisha b'Av* from its liturgical calendar marking all other Jewishly tragic events.

14. *Encyclopedia Judaica*, vol. 8, He-Ir, #1344.

7

Israel and Zionism
in the Post-*Shoah* World

Among the post-World War II and post-Auschwitz responses of
the Jewish people to the *Shoah* has been the intense energy
expended upon the reestablished State of Israel as well as the devout
Zionist commitments of Jews throughout the world toward ensuring
its survival. And, although the lobbying efforts of the early post-1948
Zionists asserted that the *only* valid Jewish life worth living is that
which is lived in Israel, the overwhelming majority of Jews continue
to not only live outside the State of Israel, but never have nor ever will
visit the Land of Israel. Along with this reality, it must be noted that, in
the forty-six years of her existence, more Israelis have undergone
yeridah (emigration *from* Israel) than American Jews have made
aliyah (immigration *to* Israel). My concerns in this chapter, however,
are neither the political nor historical dimensions of contemporary
Israel, but rather its theological ones.

After the *Shoah*, it seems to me, there are four interwoven religio-theological issues, each of which impinges upon the other and
each of which has more or less been "ignored" by the various religious
communities of Jews.[1] They are (1) a religious response to the whole
question of *yeridah* versus *aliyah*; (2) the question of the *power* of
the Jewish State and its Jewish inhabitants versus those who are not
Jews and who do not wish to live under the Israeli flag or be ruled by
its governmental apparatus; (3) the role, place, function of a religious
philosophy of Zionism, that is, whether Israel is a central or peripheral
focus of religious Judaism; and by extension, (4) whether Judaism
itself after the *Shoah* can or must affirm a nationalistic component or
is, now, in truth, transnational by definition. Each of these issues and
concerns is theologically, religiously, and emotionally complex and
fraught with danger and uncomfortability.

Given the affirmation of *chofshi*, freedom, for all Jews, both
inside and outside Israel, to live the kinds of Jewish lives they posi-

tively wish to affirm after the *Shoah*, without the imposition of an externally imposed human or Divine authority structure and without recourse to an historically traditional understanding of the Jewish religious faith, heritage, and tradition, it would be theologically and religiously absurd to affirm *aliyah* except for those who, freely, wish to do so—or those under oppressive regimes for whom *aliyah* represents their best change for "salvation" from physical, cultural, or religious genocide. Equally, guilt for not electing *aliyah*, therefore, must *not* be forced upon either Israelis who elect *yeridah*, American or other Western Jews who choose not to make *aliyah*, or those fleeing oppression who, once free, now elect to live as Jews elsewhere.

To be sure, the issue of *aliyah*, however, is not so simply addressed as just stated. *Aliyah* continues to remain the very life's blood of Israel and her Jewish population. Realistically and honestly, not reproducing her Jews in any appreciable numbers, 3.5 to 4 million Jews will not counterbalance more than 70 million Arab neighbors, not even taking into consideration Israel's indigenous non-Jewish Arab population.[2] And although *aliyah* is to be encouraged among all facets of the Jewish religious community, and positively affirmed as a viable option for all Jews, present and future, it *must* remain one option among many after the *Shoah* but not the only one.

Such thinking, however, does *not* absolve those Jews who do not elect *aliyah* from their responsibilities to *actively* support Israel economically and politically and to visit this "modern miracle of the Middle East" as often as circumstances permit. *No Jew alive after the Shoah can morally, ethically or religiously refrain from calling himself or herself a Zionist regardless of where he or she chooses to live. Indeed, if anything, the reverse is now the case: after the Shoah and the destruction of one-third to one-half of all Jews alive during the years 1939-1945, not to mention future births, all Jews have in fact become Zionists by virtue of their continuing Jewish existence and Jewish affirmations.*

Secondarily, but nonetheless significantly, the Jewish people worldwide, although by and large continuing to affirm its Zionist commitments, has not chosen to make *aliyah* its highest priority. It has, however, continued to affirm *religious* Judaism as its highest priority. Thus, honesty compels us to accept the obvious conclusion presented by the evidence: *The "saving reality" of post-Shoah Jewish life lies in its transnational character. One can be a religious Jew anywhere one is free to practice Judaism; and that very freedom leads to diverse interpretations, understandings, and redefinitions, some more and some less inclusive than others.*[3] Thus, post-*Shoah*

Judaism and post-*Shoah* Jews affirm the transnational character of both their Judaism and their Jewish selves.

Second, myths and countermyths punctuate and puncture the history of Israel's relationship with both her Arab neighbors and her indigenous Arab population. Rights and wrongs have been committed on both sides historically and contemporarily. Israel is a fact and way of life in the Middle East, and peace will ultimately come when her neighbors accept this fact and begin the connection of diplomatic relations as Egypt has already done. Israel, too, now confronted with the growing realization that there resides within her borders a significantly large indigenous "Palestinian"⁴ Arab population with equally valid claims, who do not wish to remain ruled either by an administrative apparatus or governmental structure into which it has no meaningful input, must ultimately make its own peace with the future reality of a separate "Palestinian state." Out of at times paranoiac concerns for her safety and security, Israel *has* abused the very governmental, military, and economic power of which the Jewish people has been the victimized recipients down through the centuries. And her neighbors *have* been guilty of both terrorist and genocidal acts designed to remove the nation-state of Israel from the community of nations. And those inside Israel *have* been guilty of terrorist and other violent acts that, even out of frustration, bring them shame not honor.

Now, after the *Shoah*, Jewish Israel must conform to a higher standard of ethical, moral, and religious conduct, not because the external and outside world expects it of us, but because we expect it of ourselves. Because we were made to be strangers in German, Poland, Russia, and throughout most of Europe and suffered the horrific consequences of such "otherness," Israel can ill afford to conduct itself toward any group of people as if they themselves were the outsiders. Power does corrupt and absolute power does corrupt absolutely; neither Jews outside of Israel nor Jews inside of Israel responsible for the administration of power can continue that abuse of power of which too many are guilty. What is right is right for everyone; what is wrong is wrong for everyone. Double standards for Jews and Arabs inside Israel, governmentally, economically, politically, militarily, leads, again, to strangeness, distance, otherness, and ultimately worse.

Saying this, I do not mean to theologically or religiously minimize or dismiss the realistic concerns of many, many Israelis with safety and security. Terrorist attacks are akin to rape with concomitant feelings of vulnerabilty, physical assault, and insecurity. *With the advent of nuclear capabilities, however, realistically, the safety and*

*security of the sovereign State of Israel is no longer at issue: Israel is
as safe as any nation protected by its nuclear arsenal and endan-
gered by the presence of nuclear weapons.* The violent attacks by
individuals and small groups, coming both from within and without,
will be ended only after the implementation of diplomatic relations
and the establishment of a sovereign sister state. Even then, sadly and
tragically, such attacks may never be ended, any more than they are in
any other country, but they *will* be minimized as the rationale for
them diminishes. The moral and ethical posture of Israel is the main
concern and focus of these comments.

Again, the State of Israel, this Jewish dream realized after the
Shoah, *must* serve as that *mercaz ruchani* ("spiritual center") of
which Ahad Ha-Am spoke so longer ago: a place where Jews come for
nourishment and sustenance, returning to their countries of origin
and residence if that is their desire, or fulfilling their own destinies as
Jews by remaining if that is their desire. This "hub of the Jewish
wheel," whose spokes radiate outward to all Jewish communities
throughout the world, *does* bear a special measure of responsibility to
serve as the best and brightest Jewish beacon of which it is capable
for all Jews throughout the world. That is the special blessing of living
in a reborn Jewish state after a lapse of 2,000 years. That is the special
opportunity of this Third Jewish Commonwealth: to teach our Jewish
people after the *Shoah* that the soul of our collective Jewish people
has not also died in the ovens and gas chambers that mar the landscape of Europe, thankfully now nonfunctioning. To live in Israel
today, after the *Shoah*, opens the door to the sacred possibility of,
again, living Jewish life in accord with the highest dictates of our
ethico-moral religious tradition, at all levels of society, welcoming
all, Jews and non-Jews alike, who wish to share the dream.[5]

Third, theologically and religiously, the responses of the various denominational groupings to a "religious philosophy of Zionism"
have been somewhat limited: from a fundamentalist and rejectionist
Orthodox anti-Zionist condemnation of the "secular state" wherein
the "hand of the Messiah" is absent, to that of Conservative,
Reconstructionist and Reform Jews who religiously affirm the validity
of a reborn State of Israel while continuing to struggle for their own
religious legitimacy in Israel herself, to an enlightened Orthodoxy,
all-too-often "shouted down" by their more strident and diffident
brothers, willing to work together with the secularists and their non-
Orthodox coreligionists in realizing an Israel home to all of the Jewish
people. Thankfully, what has *not* been affirmed, as noted at the end of
the last chapter, has been the obscene theological position that

regards the *Shoah* as either the necessary or sufficient condition without which the ages-old dream of the birth of this Third Jewish
Commonwealth could not have come into being.

A meaningful religious philosophy of Zionism that takes into
consideration the realities of the *Shoah* is likewise demanded today
and, by extension, an answer to the question of Israel's centrality or
peripherality in that philosophy. My own central credo of faith after
the *Shoah* can be expressed quite simply: "Without Jews, there will
be no religious Judaism; without religious Judaism (however interpreted, defined or redefined), there will be no Jews." Therefore, as a
post-*Shoah* Zionist, my religious Zionism grows out of my religious
Judaism and not the other way around; it is *not* either my excuse or
my substitute for my religious Judaism, but part of it, however central
at times I wish to make it. Under no circumstances does it replace my
commitment to a religiously meaningful life cycle and holiday-cycle
calendar nor a commitment to creative Jewish survival worldwide.
Thus, at times, especially in times of crises, my Zionist commitments
may overshadow my other Jewish commitments and rise to a place of
centrality; at other times, it recedes into a place of peripherality, as
other, equally valid parts of my religious Judaism asset themselves.
Taken together, they form my religious Judaism, no part more precious or sacred than the whole. Thus, at times, Israel after the *Shoah*
is both: central to my Jewish religious self-identity and self-awareness
and peripheral to my Jewish religious self-identity and self-awareness.
Any other conclusion or any other balancing between the two
becomes a distortion of both religious Judaism and religious Zionism.
This *religious* philosophy of Zionism thus leads directly to the fourth
and final concern of this chapter: whether Judaism post-*Shoah* is, in
fact, transnational, as already noted or can be understood only refocused on Israel and its Zionist impulse.

Whatever else we may say of Nazism and National Socialism,
the ultimate statement of its meaning is that of nationalism gone awry,
perverted in the extreme, linking, in German, *blut und boden*, "blood
and soil," into a nationalistic frenzy that polarized its own world
between "Aryan" and Jew" and resulted in the *Shoah*. Recognizing
this simple fact forces us, equally, to recognize that nationalism,
almost by definition, contains within itself the malignant seeds of
genocidal destruction of weaker subpopulations, to use Richard
Rubenstein's and Helen Fein's phrase, "outside the universe of moral
obligation." It would, therefore, be only the most naive among us
who would argue that all *other* nationalisms possess such seeds but
Jewish or *Israeli* nationalism does not.[6] The point is not whether all

such expressions of nationalism, Jewish or other, should contain such seeds, but that they do. The inherent danger, therefore, is to place oneself or one's country into this "us versus them" mind set that, in turn, leads to abuse. The responsibility is, therefore, twofold: (1) to recognize the potential and actual dangers that flow from nationalism unchecked, and (2) to guard against the abuse of state power through whatever means available, public opinion, legal system, and so on.

What this ultimately means, therefore, for a post-*Shoah* religious philosophy of Judaism, including a religious philosophy of Zionism, is a much, much more inclusive understanding of Jews and Judaism than perhaps ever before in our history. Essentially, we come full circle, almost to the point of David Ben-Gurion's famous definition of a Jew as "anyone who considers himself such." Israel and *aliyah* become one of a series of possible Jewish commitments for those Jews who elect them as such, but not the apex or zenith of post-*Shoah* Jewish commitment. Israel, perhaps more than ever before, plays an important part in the life of post-*Shoah* Jews and Judaism; it does not, however, play the dominant or dominating part, any more than any other aspect of Judaism plays such a role. Religious Judaism is now seen as an affirmation of both the holiday-cycle and life-cycle calendars and, in turn, creatively looks for ways to include in its affirmations, observances, practices, and understandings the widest possible groups of Jews individually and collectively. Israel and Zionism become a concrete and very real and important part of a renewed and revitalized religious philosophy of post-*Shoah* Judaism; they do not become, however, other than at very specific times, the central focus of that new understanding.

Last, therefore, if Jews are to be free outside of Israel to make Jewish and Israeli-related decisions, then, inside Israel, we, too, must be free to make similar decisions. *After the Shoah, it is no longer morally, ethically, or religiously acceptable for Israel to be governed in the laws of ishut (personal status) by a rigid Orthodox interpretation of halakhah (Jewish law) narrowly interpreted to exclude rather than include.* Denial of Jewish religious legitimacy to non-Orthodox interpretations and understandings of Judaism, as well as secular-humanistic interpretations and understandings, with either the official "imprimatur" of the state or the closed-blind eye thereof, are no longer acceptable nor have they ever been so. Silence in the face of supposed security threats will not serve the cause of Israel nor forge that partnership with American and any other Jewry and Israeli Jewry to be noted. Nor does the argument of the lack of historical numbers of non-Orthodox Jews bring honor and glory to Israel.

After the *Shoah*, as before, what is right, moral, and proper is just because it is right, moral, and proper and, therefore, just. Any practice of Judaism or Jews, both inside Israel and elsewhere, that excludes, for whatever reason, is both immoral and unjust. Inside Israel, the dream realized after the *Shoah*, that simply cannot be.

A final thought is appropriate here. As a religious Jew and a religious Zionist living in the United States, part of whose family continues to live in Israel, there *does* exist a special relationship between Israel and her Jewish citizenry and the American Jewish community, the largest numerically, economically, and politically "at home" Jewish community in the world resident in the sole remaining "superpower." American Jewry is not, nor has it ever been or ever will be, exclusively a ready source for *aliyah*, made to feel guilty for not yet have done so; nor is it an unlimited "checkbook" for Israel to do whatever, whenever, and wherever its current political-governmental leadership chooses to do, with the appropriate dollar amounts to be filled in later; nor is it the political lobbying arm of "official Israel," taking its instructions and direction from those in charge. Its strength is as an *equal partner* with Israel, now the two largest and most significant communities of Jews, working together to ensure the continuing survival of the Jewish people worldwide, expending whatever resources they collectively possess and using whatever clout of which they are both capable.

We turn now to Chapter 8, to an ever more troubling and problematic arena for rethinking Jewish faith, that of the interrelationship between Jews and Christians, between Judaism and Christianity, as well as those categories of *Christian* faith that must now be rethought in light of the *Shoah*.

Notes

1. One possible reason for this ignoring may very well be the relatively short distance, even today, that we are from the *Shoah*. Another may be the critical necessity of ensuring Israel's very physical survival, now an accomplished *fact*, despite the Jeremiah-like prophets of doom both inside and outside the Jewish community. And there may be others.

2. Indeed, were *all* Jews alive in the world today to make *aliyah*, it would *not* make any *significant* difference in this demographic equation despite the obvious increase in tensions and obvious benefits to the state itself.

3. Oppression of Jews, on the other hand, leads not to diversity but to uniformity, ortho*doxy* and ortho*praxy*.

4, I choose to put the word "Palestinian" in quotes because I am not at all convinced that this is the best term to describe those native Arabs who do not wish to be governed by the Israelis and whose claims to the land itself are equally valid and equally of long-standing. Not all but some.

5, The admittance of so large a number of non-Jews from the West as to "threaten" the very Jewishness of the State of Israel is unrealistic in our time. Those who presently opt for living there do so *because* of its very Jewishness and Jewish character.

6. Sadly enough, we have already seen during the years of the Arab-Palestinian *intifada* abuses of state power.

Addendum

The "historic handshake" between Israeli Prime Minister Yitzhak Rabin and PLO Chairperson Yasir Arafat, following the signing of the "Declaration of Principles on Interim Self-Government Arrangements" in Washington, DC, on 13 September 1993, in the presence of President Bill Clinton, Secretary of State Warren Christopher, Israeli Foreign Minister Shimon Peres, and PLO Executive Committee member Mahmoud Abbas, does *not* change the focus of this chapter. "Cautious optimism" continues to be present in the Jewish communities of both Israel and the United States, as well as throughout the world. The 'sina qua non' of this Agreement will be the commitment of the PLO towards guaranteeing and participating in the safety and security of the State of Israel and the willingness of additional Arab nation-states to enter into peaceful agreements and negotiations with Israel. [The signing of the "Israeli-Jordan Agenda" by Israeli chief negotiator Elyakim Rubenstein and Jordanian chief negotiator Fayez Tarawneh at the State Department, Washington, DC, on 14 September 1993, is such a first step.]

A cautionary note: Only the most naive among us, it seems to me, would regard the signing of the above 'Arrangements' as *not*, ultimately, leading to the creation of an independent sovereign Palestinian State in the not-too-distant future. What this will mean in concrete detail will be the coming confrontation between Israel and her neighbors. Likewise the continuing issues surrounding the city of Jerusalem. Such a creation, however, does *not* absolve Israel and the Jewish People, both within and without, of their responsibilities inside Israel towards her non-Jewish citizens.

Theologically and religiously, what the reality of two sovereign nation-states, an Israeli state and a Palestinian state side-by-side, means may very well be a rethought understanding for Jews *and Arabs* of the "other." At this point, we will have to wait and see what the ensuing years bring.

8

Rethinking Christianity:
An Outsider's Perspective

Orthodox Rabbi and thinker Eliezer Berkovits in *Faith After the Holocaust*[1] tells the story of a rabbi survivor of the *Shoah* who was confronted after World War II by a sincere, devout, and well-meaning Christian layperson who asked him, "What do you want from us now that the war is over?" The rabbi is said to have responded, "All we want from you is that you keep your hands off our children!"

His response, whether apocryphal or not, is indicative of the terribly sad and tragic state to which Jewish-Christian relations had deteriorated both prior to and during the *Shoah* as well as historically. Even today, now five decades after the events of 1933(39)-1945, Jewish-Christian relations continues to be a house fragilely built, at times strong in the face of adversarial attacks, for example, synagogue desecrations by the KKK, neo-Nazis, skinheads, and other racists; and weak at other times, for example, the lack of response to the continuing assassination of Israel in the various media. Living predominantly in a non-Jewish, Christian, Western world after the *Shoah*, Christianity itself, as well as Jewish-Christian relations, are topics worthy of theological exploration by both Jews and Christians. It is one of the premises of this book that, after Auschwitz, the *Jewish* theological categories of God, covenant, prayer, *halakhah* and *mitzvot*, life cycle, holiday cycle, and Israel and Zionism *must* be rethought because the historically traditional understanding of those categories no longer applies. By extension, therefore, if we are truthful and honest with ourselves, as Jews and as Christians, *Christian* theological categories, too, must be rethought and reevaluated.

Though it obviously would be somewhat presumptuous for one who is not a Christian to elaborate all those categories of faith central to the Christian religious experience that now must be rethought and reevaluated in light of the *Shoah*, such an agenda must be presented *to* the Christian communities *by* the Christian communities and *for* the Christian communities. Preliminarily, the following four categories as well as the further elaboration of those suggested are, realistically and honestly, better left to Christian philosophers and theologians, better equipped by virtue of their own training, education, and commitment to grapple with their implications. In addition, now, more than ever, serious, studious, open, and honest dialogue *must* be pursued between Jews and Christians, not to erase the past but to understand it and chart new directions away from its repetition and continuation.

For Christians, it seems to me, what must be rethought are (1) the whole notion of God the Father and His Son Jesus the Redeeming Christ in an unredeemed world that could and did countenance the *Shoah*; (2) the very "mission" of the church specifically toward the Jewish people and generally towards all non-Christian peoples in the aftermath of the *Shoah*, as well as toward each other; (3) the proper relationship between the "parent" Judaism and the "child" Christianity, between Jews and Christians, given the long, sad, and tragic history of that relationship, or, rather, nonrelationship; and (4) a long, hard look at the historical realities and implications of the relationship between Jews and Christians, beginning with the birth of Christianity and the person of Paul and including the rise of Nazism, all *before* turning to our contemporary world.

Prior to doing so, however, comment must be made regarding the supposed "antisemitism" of the New Testament itself.[2]

To condemn the New Testament as "antisemitic," it seems to me, is both to misread and misunderstand the text and *tendenz* of the anti-Judaic portrait painted therein. A much more accurate understanding of that negative depiction would be to see the controversy as "in-house, intrafamily Jewish debate and dispute," with the Gospel of John excepted, being an attack on the Jews by one outside the family, later taken over by the non-Jewish, gentile successors to Paul, who, in their burgeoning desire both to separate themselves from their Jewish beginnings and further to create a new and distinct *religious* response to the times, lost sight of the original *meaning* of those words, with disastrous future results.

Saying this, however, does not absolve the Christian faithful from reading and understanding the New Testament properly *in its own historical context* in the early rabbinic period. Much important scholarly work has already been done in this area with more yet to be done.[3]

Nor does it absolve the Christian faithful from grappling with a far more profound textual problem than that of a lack of a true and accurate historical understanding; namely, recognizing that one's sacred and centrally precious literature contains within it statements historically negative and prejudicial toward Jews and contemporarily affirmed and reaffirmed, what does one *do* with the New Testament text, first liturgically, and second educationally and theologically? For example, does one, church or individual, simply excise those problematic passages from the liturgical and lectionary calendars, relegating them to the questionable status of "forbidden sweets," shrouding them with an aura of mystery and secrecy which, perversely, heightens their appeal? Does one, church or individual, *retranslate* those same passages so that the language itself is more reflective of an increased historical understanding, with copious footnotes and comments to be sure? Is such even possible? Does one, church or individual, rerank the educational and theological agenda of Christianity making these painfully difficult passages the "new curriculum" for the 1990s and beyond?

As a Jew and an outsider, I do not know the answers to these questions. I know only that the place to start this reexamination of Christianity and Jewish-Christian relations is with the text of the New Testament itself, before turning to the four areas that form the substance of my comments in this chapter. Thankfully, that work has already been done; what has not yet happened, in the main, is the "filtering down" of that importance research into the pews of the various churches and denominations nor, in many cases, into the curricula of the seminaries and training and continuing education of clergy. After the *Shoah*, morally, it seems to me, the various Christian communities have a fundamental and primary responsibility to present their sacred New Testament text to their adherents with all of its problems, difficulties, and implications already in evidence in the text itself. This should be done with all the honesty and skill of which they are capable. Only then can a foundation for bridge-building between Jews and Christians be solidly presented.

Having said this, let us now turn to the first of these four difficult areas of a rethought Christianity: that of the *Redeeming* Christ versus an *unredeemed* world where a *Shoah* was not only possible but actual.

It is my understanding of Christianity that, whatever else we may say of Jesus the Christ, his atoning death on the cross, his *willingness* to offer up his own life in place of pitiable and pitiful humanity, spared it further degradation in the sight of God and *redeemed* it from sin and death forever and all time. That is to say, in other words, that the world and humanity have, somehow, mysteriously, been for-

ever and irrevocably "changed" by this singularly unique act by a singularly unique individual who was "more than" simply a human being
but represented *in his person* the merging of both the Divine and
the human in a way never before offered to humanity or ever again to
be replicated.

Jewishly, after the *Shoah*, in addition to all of the obvious difficulties in explaining the Trinity and trinitarianism to a community
for whom Monotheism is understood to mean one, singular,
unique, indivisible by any other number or understanding, whose
own understanding of Messiah is that of a charismatic human being
of leadership qualities superior to the ordinary individual but a
human being nonetheless, one question looms larger than any
other: *Where or how* was or is the world *redeemed* after the Christ?
How has the world *changed* after the Christ, given 2,000 years of,
at times, Christian oppression of Jews through expulsion, ghettoization, forced conversion, and extermination-annihilation? How
does the Christ's *redemption* of the world square with a *Shoah*
that saw the deaths of 6 million Jews, 1 million innocent children
below the age of 12, and an additional 500,000 young people if
we raise the age to 18? Not to mention 5 million non-Jews,
Christians included?

Theologically, is it logical to say that the world was, indeed,
"redeemed" by and after the death of the Christ, but that the world,
humanity, continues to ignore its own redemption? Or is it more logical to say that the world was *potentially redeemed* by the death of
the Christ on the cross, a potential that continues to exist for the
world, which up to now, has refused to welcome that potential into
its midst? Is it not, therefore, also logical to suggest that the Christ represents *for those who choose him*, the paradigmatic model of the
very best of which humanity is capable: to surrender one's life out of
love for another, examples of which are, also, to be found in the
"righteous gentiles" and Jews of the *Shoah*, realizing all the while
that the actual death of the Christ did *not*, either at that moment or up
to this moment, redeem our world, but only opened the door to that
possibility?[4]

Having now Jewishly understood the birth, death, and "resur-
rection," again a theological faith claim about which we disagree and
will continue to disagree, as redemptive only in their potential, we
turn to the second of the four questions of a rethought Christianity
after the *Shoah*: that of its missionizing thrust not only to the Jewish
people first but to all non-Christians as well as to those within the
Christian community.

The so-called great commission of the Gospel tradition, as I understand it, is the *obligation* incumbent upon *all* Christians of whatever denominational stripe to "share the 'Good News' of Jesus the Christ with all those whom are not yet Christians." To be sure, such sharing is to occur out of genuine love and caring for non-Christians and a sincere and heartfelt desire for them to share in the afterlife as Christianity understands it. Overzealousness to do so, down through the centuries as well as contemporarily, has, unfortunately, negated those positive emotions and feelings that stem from a secure religious faith and commitment and led to further estrangement between Jews and Christians.

For religiously sensitive Jews after the *Shoah* attempting to rebuild shattered lives and families, committed to building the Third Jewish Commonwealth in the State of Israel, such missionizing was and remains morally offensive to the point of repugnance. Having suffered so much because we were Jews, having called into question so much of previously accepted Jewish religious faith, heritage, and tradition because of the *Shoah*, the answer to our pain is not that of surrender to another religious tradition. After all, Hitler and his minions refused to accept religious conversion, even of the previous two generations, as valid exemptions from the "final solution." Therefore, in the minds of many Jews, such "sharing of the Gospel" has even been perceived as furthering the work of the Nazis.

Better *now* for *all* segments of the Christian world, morally and ethically, to accept the following: After the *Shoah*, Christianity remains an option for all those, Jews included, who are willing to explore its possibilities and its potential and come to it without coercion. But to aggressively promote its proselytizing and conversionary activities as the only and exclusive way to experience the Divine-human encounter, however understood and interpreted, is to express no love or caring for Jews, to build no bridges between the child-faith community and its parent. Better now to accept the stated fact that individuals and families and groups in a post-Auschwitz world *must* be *free* to pursue their own destinies, religious and other, as they perceive them, provided these destinies do not impinge on their neighbors nor do violence or injustice to them.

Also, in those cases where a significant loving and caring relationship between a Jew and a Christian already exists, there is nothing offensive on the part of the Christian friend who desires to share that which is centrally precious in his or her religious life, recognizing fully two things: (1) after such sharing, that relationship may very well be dramatically altered, and (2) the Jewish recipient is free *not* to

act upon such knowledge. Textually, Christian scholars and preach-
ers, therefore, must rethink and reject their former understanding of
those Gospel passages that command the conversion of the Jews and,
by extension, other non-Christian religious adherents. It is one thing
to say that "There are passages in our own New Testament, our sacred
literature, that command us to convert the Jews." It is quite something
else to admit their historical relevance and applicability, but now,
because of changed historical circumstances, the *Shoah* to be specific, to have the courage to reject them as contemporarily meaningful. Christianity remains a worthwhile religious option in our post-
Shoah world, as does Judaism, Islam, Buddhism, Hinduism, or what
have you. It does not, however, remain the only viable religious possibility.

By extension, therefore, what has just been written down about
the relationship between Christianity and Judaism after the *Shoah* is
equally applicable to the relationship between Christianity and other,
non-Jewish, religious traditions. Conversion, other than involuntary
and coercive, always remains a possibility, but not the only possibility.
And within its own house and own family, too, conversion must be
rethought: More appropriate in our post-*Shoah* and post-Auschwitz
world is to now acknowledge the validity of the "covenants of dialogue" as explicitly stated in Chapter 2, "Covenant: Involuntary?
Voluntary? Nonexistent?" than to continue to falsely perceive the
world in an adversarial "we versus you" relationship, that is, in reality,
an antirelationship.

What then now becomes the "right and proper" relationship
between Judaism and Christianity, between Jews and Christians, after
and in light of the *Shoah*? Initially, two points bear on any such discussion: (1) Evolving Christianity *does* bear a measure of responsibility and culpability for the *Shoah*, for without such recognition of
such responsibility and culpability little dialogue will take place
between Jews and Christians;[5] and (2) Christianity itself, coming out
of the very loins of Judaism, is indebted to Judaism and must ever be
respectful of both its parent- faith and its origins and beginnings. For
Jews, in addition, what must now be recognized if the dialogue is to
move forward are the following: (1) Despite its long, sad, and tragic
past, contemporary Christianity and contemporary Christians are *not*,
in general, the enemies of Judaism and the Jewish people;[6] and (2) following the Talmud's own understanding of Christianity as a monotheism, albeit a most peculiar one from Judaism's perspective, that "the
righteous of all nations will have a share in the world to come," a far
healthier Jewish understanding of Christianity would be possible,

that is, to see Christianity as a *midrashic* interpretation of religious Judaism, one whose roots remain deep within the Jewish religious tradition, and one whose activist appeal to those not born into the Jewish community remains strong and powerful. Its religio-theological message, as well as its ethico-moral positions, likewise find their origins within Judaism. Initially resentful of its parent, Christianity continues to evolve toward a maturing relationship with Judaism, not yet there but moving forward. Such movement must continue.

As I have written elsewhere, the uniqueness of Nazi antisemitism is its "biological-racial" basis; it is the "end" of an antisemitic journey that begins in pre-Christian Egypt, Greece, and Rome with a cultural-social manifestation of antisemitism *through* Christian religious and theological antisemitism to a European Enlightenment and post-Enlightenment political antisemitism to the biological antisemitism of National Socialism. During the so-called Christian period from the birth of Christianity to the Enlightenment, the relationship or nonrelationship between Jews and Christians, in the main, most pointedly after Christianity allied itself with the political machinations of the "Holy" Roman Empire and beyond, took one or more of four possible forms: (1) removal of Jews from the physical environs where we had lived for hundreds if not thousands of years, explusion; (2) being allowed to remain but in restricted settlement areas, ghettoization; (3) being allowed to remain but only upon surrendering of Jewish identity and the adoption of Christian identity, forced conversion; (4) being put to death because we were Jews with no recourse to escape through bribery or whatever, extermination-annihilation.[7]

Additionally, Paul's own ambivalence towards his Jewish religious system and roots, as manifested in so many New Testament passages, continues to result in continuing ambivalence toward Jews and Judaism even today. Again, the New Testament text is the place to start, carefully plumbing its depths and examining closely, historically, linguistically, theologically, *all* those passages, Paul's and others especially the four Gospel writers, which *directly* and *indirectly* address Jews and Judaism. Having done so, the "story" of the resulting relationship must now, after the *Shoah*, be taught in churches and seminaries, in colleges and universities, if we are to build the kind of bridges between our two faith communities that I am now suggesting are appropriate in our post-*Shoah* and post-Auschwitz world.

Why so? For two reasons: particularistically, as a Jew concerned with the survival of my own Jewish people and my own family, as the child of a survivor-refugee, himself now deceased, whose own family lost more than 150 members, I do not want a repetition of this nightmarish tragedy to revisit us. And, universally, in a nuclear world capable of both genocide and omnicide, German Pastor Martin Niemoeller's oft-quoted statement rings aloud with new clarity and urgency.[8] Our world grows continually smaller and more interdependent economically, ecologically, and politically; the threat of universal destruction ecologically, militarily, nuclearly likewise remains an ever-present dark shadow upon planet earth. Recognition of our common need to enter into "covenants of dialogue" for our own mutually assured survival becomes paramount. After the *Shoah*, it has become morally, ethically, religiously, and theologically imperative that Jews and Judaism and Christians and Christianity demonstrate, by their commitment to overcoming their past, the potential for goodness and shared respect that yet remains in both the present and the future. I hope, before it is too late, it is a demonstration from which all can learn.

We come now to the last chapter in this initial exploration of rethinking Jewish faith after the *Shoah*. At best, it is a summary of what has been previously written, pointing us toward a theological dialogue that has yet to take place stripped of all the heightened emotionalism and steadfast clinging to the past which has produced far more heat than light. That this volume has somehow contributed to that dialogue is more than ample repayment for the anguish it produced though never for the historical events that called it into being.

Notes

1. New York: Ktav Publishing House, 1973.

2. Here I am somewhat indebted to the writings and teachings of both Ellis Rivkin and the late Samuel Sandmel, *alav hashalom*, among others.

3. The writings of James Charlesworth, Paula Frederiksen, John P. Meier, Jacob Neusner, Sharon H. Ringe, E. P. Sanders, Elizabeth Schussler-Fiorenza, John Townsend, and Clark Williamson come readily to mind.

4. The question of the Divine-human nature of the Christ is not one to be explored here for the obvious reason that this is a primary faith claim of Christianity, growing as it does out of the New Testament text, interpretively affirmed according to its own understanding by the Hebrew Scriptures, a faith claim that is *not* in accord with a Jewish understanding of either God or the messiah. At best, perhaps, all we can say is that it is one of those religiously sensitive areas about which we agree to disagree and always shall do so.

5. We need not be reminded in this context that historic antisemitism and whatever vestiges still remain *are* a blot on contemporary Christianity.

6. Again, the "righteous gentiles" of the *Shoah* are the beginning refutation of such thinking; after all, many of them did what they did to save Jews out of their commitments *as Christians*. The French village of Le Chambon, as detailed by Philip Hallie in his *Lest Innocent Blood Be Shed: The Story of the Village of Le Chambon and How Goodness Happened There* (New York: Harper and Row, 1979), is one such example.

7. Raul Hilberg's threefold schema, again, appears relevant: "You have no right to live among us as Jews" to "You have no right to live among us" to "You have no right to live." See his magisterial work, *The Destruction of the European Jews*, revised and definitive ed. (New York: Holmes and Meier, 1985), 3 vols., for his presentation of this thesis. Also, one need only read Roman Catholic Father Edward Flannery's *The Anguish of the Jews: Twenty-Three Centuries of Antisemitism* (New York: Paulist Press, 1985), among others, to give concrete evidence of this tragic story.

8. "In Germany, they came first for the Communists, and I didn't speak up because I wasn't a Communist. Then they came for the Jews, and I didn't speak up because I wasn't a Jew. Then they came for the trade unionists and I didn't speak up because I wasn't a trade unionist. Then they came for the Catholics, and I didn't speak up because I was a Protestant. Then they came for me, and by that time, nobody was left to speak up."

9

Summarizing:
Is Such Even Possible?

The time for Jewish and Christian guilt and accusation is long past. To include among us only those who are now willing to maintain past structures and past religious rationalizations subsequent to the *Shoah* is equally as pernicious as excluding those who no longer wish to do so. What is of primary relevance and importance are those Jews and Christians who, *freely*, are willing to practice those forms of historically traditional behaviors and non-historically traditional behaviors that they themselves find meaningful, out of their genuine desire to commit themselves to the Jewish or Christian people and future and to the God who may be seen as having had *something* to do with their origins. The "bottom line" must be our willingness to make those commitments rather than the standards by which any subgroup of Jews or Christians chooses to evaluate the totality of its membership and include or exclude. To impose guilt upon those who no longer think and act in accord with the ways of the past is to deny both the present and the future. Our refocused religious and theological agendas must now be inclusive rather than exclusive if our world is to maintain any sense of equilibrium and survive, given the contemporary pressures with which it is currently confronted, and in that process, make room for the Jewish children of *Shoah* survivors and their descendants. To this end, I have chosen to examine those categories of Jewish faith that suggest themselves to me as primary: God, covenant, prayer, *halakhah* and *mitzvot*, life cycle, festival cycle, Israel and Zionism, Christianity, and Jewish-Christian relations.

In my Introduction, after having shared something of my autobiography, I focused on the *rationale* for this book: The *fact* that the *Shoah* presents enormous theological problems for one committed to a viable religious tradition. All those who have thus far addressed these difficulties, however, have either been survivors themselves or contemporaneous with the survivors, Jewish or Christian. *None of those who have thus far addressed these theological conundrums have themselves been members of the "Second Generation," we children of survivors.* Additionally and fundamentally, these same Jewish and Christian theologians have primarily chosen to address the broader themes, the "big picture," rather than the specifics of life cycle and festival cycle; that is, how one *does* Judaism and Christianity after the *Shoah.* Each of the aforementioned "categories of concern" is addressed here in terms of the questions I do truly believe need to be answered for a post-*Shoah*, post-Auschwitz religious philosophy of Judaism. Each of these categories has proven itself worthy of a separate chapter, as I have done, though, obviously, all are interrelated and intertwined. I conclude this introductory chapter by giving my own personal rationale for remaining within the Jewish fold as I initially attempt to answer the questions I raise, committed as I am to a Judaism *free* of externally imposed authority or historically traditional reasons. Having said all of this, my hope and prayer continue to be that, somehow, this book will further contribute to a dialogue about the kind of post-*Shoah* Judaism which can speak meaningfully to Jews today, a dialogue only recently begun.

In Chapter 1, "The Problem with God," the very *absence* of God during the *Shoah* presents both the greatest difficulty and the greatest challenge to contemporary Judaism and Jews and Christianity and Christians. What I urge, therefore, based on the historical evidence of the *Shoah* is an understanding of a *limited* God, not a historically traditional one, which accepts that Divine absence or Divine impotence, acknowledges the reality of radical evil in our world, and accepts equally the reality of human freedom for good or evil. Implicit in this urging is, likewise, an acceptance of the very uniqueness of the *Shoah* itself with all that such uniqueness implies. For me, therefore, the understanding of a limited and limiting God that makes the most sense is that of a Creator God, *Borei Olam*, who, in the very process of creation, erected an impenetrable barrier between Himself or Herself and creation. *Human tragedy, therefore, the Shoah included, is fully, totally, and completely the result of human action or inaction. After creation, we human beings are, ultimately and absolutely, responsible for the past, present, and future of this planet and for the populations that reside on it.*

Theologically and religiously, as well as liturgically, therefore, our initial response to this understanding of God is that of recognition, acknowledgment and thanksgiving, all the while keeping in mind that such responses are *not* communicated beyond the confines of this planet.

Chapter 2, "Covenant: Involuntary? Voluntary? Non-Existent?" follows logically upon the back of my understanding of this limited and self-limiting God in no way responsible for the *Shoah*. As I understand our history, the Jewish understanding of *Brith* is based on the idea of the God who acts in history and is, therefore, rejected both by the evidence of Divine impotence in the face of the *Shoah* and by the historical evidence of the *Shoah* itself. *God's ultimate failure to save or protect the Jewish people during the Shoah invalidates (1) any believe in the efficacy of the Brith itself, and (2) any claim the Jewish people might otherwise have to call upon God for active involvement, including, but not limited to, intervention or rescue.* By extension, both the ideas of the "chosen people," better for me the "choosing people," and the "election of Israel" are, equally, casualties of the *Shoah*. Instead, I continue to plead for "covenants of dialogue" between all the various groupings in all of the various human configurations that presently people our planet, based upon that mutual sharing of information and ideas and the setting forth of common agendas and agreements.

Chapter 3, "The Crises of Prayer," builds upon six primary recognitions after the *Shoah*: (1) the universe *does* manifest certain harmonies if we are but receptive to them; (2) creation *does* allow us more possibilities for human growth than does destruction; (3) aesthetic appreciation of our world *does* enhance our pleasure at being part of it; (4) the prayerfully poetic words of our predecessors of both religious traditions, now reinterpreted after the *Shoah*, do likewise increase the shared yearnings of all humankind for peace and survival; (5) the disciplined gatherings of like-minded groups in celebration and in sorrow *do* help energize us to confront the challenges of our own day and learn from each other; and (6) we need not suspend our intellect nor deny historical realities, especially the *Shoah*, when we engage in what we continue to call prayer. Joined to these recognitions, therefore, are four scientific or intellectual understandings: (1) this planet is not directly headed toward either the sun or the moon, nor are other planetary bodies headed directly toward us, that is, planet earth is not immediately in danger of extinction as the result of *external* forces; (2) the rhythm of all life's existence, plant, animal, human, is birth, growth, maturation, decay, and death; (3) the things that we create are far from infinite; and (4) ideas, ideals, beliefs, and relationships are, ultimately, what sustain us and best enable us to positively move from one plane of our existence to the next.

Therefore, my starting point for any discussion of prayer in this context of post-*Shoah* Judaism is an acknowledgment of the inherent harmony of all life and expressed verbalization to that effect. Likewise, my own appreciation of the aesthetic impulse in all humanity, in all of its diverse possibilities, is linked to a freer interpretation and expression of the possibilities Jewishly than has thus far been the case. After the *Shoah*, liturgy *must* be preservative, adaptive, and innovative. Only inclusive nurturing and caring Jewish and Christian communities of faith will provide such opportunities as well as places for those of us who continue to struggle and wrestle with prayer after the *Shoah* even as the "poetry of the soul" and "moments of beauty" continue to assert themselves.

Chapter 4, "*Halakhah* and *Mitzvot*: Law and Commandments—The Heart of the Matter," suggests a *positive* reformulation of "doing" Judaism as a *disciplined* response to the perceived Divine-human and human-human encounters, cognizant always that both commandment and law are no longer religiously operative or authoritative as historically and traditionally understood. Meaningfully rethought criteria, based on *serious* Jewish study and *serious* Jewish doing, ritually and ceremonially and ethically and morally, are six: (1) intellectual, (2) aesthetic, (3) emotional, (4) physical, (5) psychological, and (6) spiritual. *What I do truly and fully believe is that contained within both the Judaism of the past and the Judaism of the present are the kernels of a viable new Jewish reality that will best enable us to affirm our Jewish selves in the most positive of ways and go forward on our life's journey, individually and collectively, in the aftermath of the Shoah.*

Chapter 5, "Rethinking the Jewish Life Cycle: From Birth to Death," and Chapter 6, "Rethinking the Jewish Festival Cycle: The Calendar in Question," are of a piece: reexamining the *specifics* of doing Judaism as they concretely manifest themselves in these two calendars by studying the various rationalizations behind their doing. In Chapter 5, the various life-cycle events are examined through the prismatic lenses of the various rabbinical manuals of the major Jewish religious movements, Orthodox, Conservative, and Reform. Here, the "bottom line" is, quite, simply, that the *Shoah* seems to have had no impact whatsoever upon the life cycle of the Jewish people as reflected in these manuals. This I regard as neither appropriate nor desired. Alternative understandings in light of the *Shoah* are given for each life-cycle moment as opposed to those historically traditional ones that continue to emphasize both covenant and commandment.

Chapter 6 groups the festival calendar holidays into four categories: (1) biblical—major; (2) biblical—minor; (3) rabbinic, and (4) contemporary. Alternative understandings are likewise supplied here in contrast to those that emphasize *brith* and *mitzvah*.

Chapter 7, "Israel and Zionism in Our Post-*Shoah* World," addresses a rethought *religious* philosophy and theology of Zionism and Israel raising four key issues: (1) *yeridah* versus *aliyah* free of the question of guilt or coercion in a post-*Shoah* world that now affirms Zionism as a badge of Jewish identity for *all* Jews; (2) *power* versus *powerlessness* and their abuse in the State of Israel by both Jewish Israelis and Arab Israelis; (3) *centrality* versus *peripherality* in a post-Auschwitz *religious* philosophy of Judaism; and (4) *nationalism* versus *transnationalism* in Judaism's understanding of itself. *I am a Jewish religious Zionist for whom Israel is both central and peripheral and who believes that only a separate Palestinian state will, ultimately, ensure the survival of Jewish Israel.*

Chapter 8, "Rethinking Christianity: An Outsider's Perspective," addresses both Christianity and Jewish-Christian relations and argues that both must be rethought after the *Shoah*. What must be examined, it seems to me, are (1) Jesus the Christ as Redeemer versus an unredeemed *Shoah*-producing world; (2) the "mission" of the church toward *all* non-Christians versus the categorical rejection of mission, the former being offensive to large numbers of Christians as well as Jews after the *Shoah*; (3) the special and unique relationship between Judaism and Christianity, recognizing both Christian culpability in some measure for the *Shoah* as well as Christianity's debt to Judaism for its own beginnings;[1] (4) the historical past, including such questions as the supposed antisemitism of the New Testament, the person of Paul, the contributions of Christianity toward a different understanding of the Divine-human and human-human encounters, and others.

The caustic query "Who died and made you God?" has been answered for some among us, especially for me, by the very deaths of the Six Million: Their deaths have forced some among us, myself included, to confront the constraints of that past and a present and future no longer bound by those constraints. Out of such a confrontation, Jews may very well come to a new synthesis of God, Torah, and Israel; and Christians may come to a new understanding of God the Father, His Son Jesus the Christ and all of humanity; and given the "new realities" of our contemporary world, Jews and Christians and Muslims may develop a new relationship beneficial to all humankind.

Note

1. Jews, however, must *always* keep in mind the comment made by Rabbi Harold Schulweis of Valley Beth Shalom Temple in Encino, California, which I first heard in 1975: "The most difficult things for Jews to remember is that not every Christian is an antisemite and not every German is a Nazi!"

Appendixes

The two appendixes (articles) included here, as well as a third—
"Judaism and Christianity After Auschwitz"[1]—form the beginnings of
my thinking about Judaism and the *Shoah* that ultimately led to this
book. To the degree, however, that I have been on this theological
journey far longer than the first publication of these pieces, two influ-
ences loom large: (1) my own growing up as outlined briefly in the
autobiographical section in the Introduction, and (2) the opportunity to spend a week in intensive study in the summer of 1967 with
Richard L. Rubenstein after the initial appearance of his seminally
foundational book, *After Auschwitz: Radical Theology and
Contemporary Judaism*.[2] It has taken me more than two decades of
reflecting, searching, and evolving to pen these words.

Notes

1. See Steven L. Jacobs, "Judaism and Christianity After Auschwitz," in
Steven L. Jacobs, ed., *Contemporary Jewish Religious Responses to the Shoah*
(Lanham, Md.: University Press of America, 1993), pages 1-21.

2. Indianapolis: The Bobbs-Merrill Company, 1966.

Appendix I:
"[If] There Is No 'Commander'? . . .
There Are No 'Commandments'!"

I

Those who know me know that, whatever else may be said of me, I am a child of the Holocaust: that the events of 1933-1945, which, at their conclusion, realized the horrendous deaths of Six Million of our own, 5 million others, and 20 million Russians, have so affected my every waking moment that everything I do, everything I say, everything I think is, somehow, colored by that Holocaust.

Specifically, I am the last surviving male member of my family to bear our name, son of an escapee, a survivor, whose entire family was unknown to me, with the exception of a very few relatives—in this country now one; in Israel two; and in South America one. Today, I teach courses on the Holocaust in all three institutions of higher learning in my community; I write and lecture in other communities; I read everything that I can about the Holocaust in an attempt to fathom the *meaning* of those events; and I am presently working on a book dealing with the implications of the Holocaust, as well as gathering material for a series of projected works on a major scholar of genocide, Dr. Raphael Lemkin. Even more specifically, my very reason for entering the rabbinate is the result of growing up the child of a survivor. Whatever else it is, my rabbinate is my *personal* answer to the tragedy of my family and our people. It is my "NO!" to Adolf Hitler, may his name be blotted out, who, fortunately, failed in his quest to make our world *Judenrein*, free of Jews. It is my "YES!" that the people Israel and the various evolutions of our faith called Judaism possess continuing viability and dynamism.

And, yet, whatever else this Holocaust has done to me as I have grown toward maturity, it has shattered for all time the easy accep-

Reprinted from *JUDAISM: A Quarterly Journal of Jewish Thought*, 37, no. 3 (Summer 1988): 323-326. Permission granted.

tance of the Jewish religious thinking that is most particularly identified with thinking about God and the just ways in which this world,
supposedly created in response to Divine desire, came to be. My family background is not Reform; generations of my German-Jewish family were Orthodox. My Grandfather, whom I never knew, may his
ashes rest in peace, was a pious Jew whose place was in his little
synagogue every Sabbath year-round. For my Father, may he rest in
peace, as best as I can express it, his Orthodoxy died in the concentration camps of Europe, amidst the ashes of his family. For the first
three decades of his life in this country, after having escaped from
Germany at the age of 18, he could not even put on a skull-cap without renewing the pain of his former experience.

All of which brings me to God. Or, perhaps, more accurately, all
of which leads me away from God—from the historical and traditional
understanding of God with which our Jewish People has long been
identified. For me, and others like me, those ideas, too, died in the
camps; they, too, are buried amidst those same ashes, in nameless
graves and countless cemeteries made sacred by the very blood of
our martyred millions.

The events of the Holocaust have shattered for me the historical
religious ideas of our Jewish people and have forced me to *rethink*
the entire process of my Jewish identity. That I have chosen the rabbinate as the vehicle wherein my thinking must take place, working
amidst our Jewish People, in addition to the college campuses where
I teach, should indicate my continual caring and commitment to the
present and future survival of our people. But I no longer believe as
did my Grandfather, killed by the Nazis, believed; I reject the God that
my Father rejected because that God, too, died in those same camps,
along with our family and our historical ideas.

Let me be even more specific: I no longer pray to a Commander
God because I do not believe that this concept is accurately reflective
of either the God of the Jewish people or of the historical experience of the Jewish people. This view bespeaks a potent, powerful
God who interacts with this planet and with the creatures who
inhabit it. It informs us that that same God truly cares about us and
what happens to us and that *His* commandments, whatever else they
are designed to do, are, ultimately, for our benefit. For me, this is
simply not so.

Shall I now, given everything that I have thus far stated, affirm a
God who "commands" me to observe "commandments" or "obligations"? Shall I lull myself into a false sense of security, comfortable
with a God who "hears prayers," when I know that my own meager

level of piety is so much less than that of my Grandfather Leo whose prayers evidently went unanswered, as did those of so many of our brothers and sisters?

Quite obviously, this I cannot do and be true to myself and to the experiences of my family and our People. What I must do, instead, is (1) *rethink* my understanding of God, God's supposed relationship with humanity, and the ways in which this God appears to function, and (2) *rethink*, and, therefore, redefine this whole concept of "commandments."

II

I am left with these alternatives: (1) Having now rejected the classical or historical or traditional Jewish understandings, I can walk out through the door; leave the Jewish people and look elsewhere to fulfill whatever spiritual needs I currently possess. Having committed myself to the rabbinate, however, to serving in the congregational rabbinate, and to the rearing of a particular Jewish family, I have obviously *not* elected this option. (2) I can redefine my understanding of God, the relationship of God to the Jewish people, and the particular concept of commandment which is our concern. Equally as obvious, therefore, I have elected, out of my strong desire and personal need, both to remain within the Jewish People and to work within that same Jewish People, this second alternative.

Therefore, let me now state my conclusion, as baldly as I can, and explain it afterwards. *For me, there is no God who is a "Commander," and, therefore, there are no "commandments" emanating from that God. Except for the exigencies of history which continue to deny us any opportunity to escape our Jewish identity, the only "commandments" which exist are those which we willingly and positively take upon ourselves out of our personal desire to be positively affirming Jews.*

The question which we must ask is, "What criteria or standards can/do we use by which to incorporate 'commandments' into our Jewish lives?" It seems to me, if we are honest and truthful with ourselves, there are six:

1. *Intellectual*: I am willing to incorporate into my Jewish behavior those historical Jewish acts which do not offend my intellectual understanding of reality and which, also, appeal to my awareness of order and precision in the universe of which I am a part. It is not that I am bound to them by some external Presence or

Force; it is, rather, that I choose to bind myself to those specifically Jewish acts which "make sense" to me. Here the rhythmic celebration of the Sabbath is the premier example.

2. *Aesthetic*: There are those Jewish acts which provide me with aesthetic pleasure: visually, orally, aurally, tactilly, and, yes, even through a sense of smell. I am, therefore, willing to do them for that reason. Examples: the spices of *Havdalah* and the citron of *Sukkot*.

3. *Emotional*: Because I am not totally a being of intellect, I have genuine emotional needs which, in turn, can be met through the doing of Jewish acts, and, therefore, I make my own commitments to their doing because they meet those needs. Being actively involved in a Jewish community is paramount for me.

4. *Physical*: There are those Jewish acts which address the very physical part of my being and ask of me certain responses which equally evoke certain positive reactions and I willingly do them for that reason. Ritual circumcision of an 8-day-old Jewish male is one example.

5. *Psychological*: In addition to my previously mentioned needs, there are psychological needs which certain "commandments" may meet, and I am likewise prepared to do them for that reason. Celebrating the Jewish calendar and Jewish life-cycle, together with my fellow-Jews, addresses those needs.

6. *Spiritual*: My own personal rejection of the historically traditional Jewish understanding of God does not, for me, negate the entire Jewish religious enterprise. I do not minimize the sense of awe and wonder at life and the universe. No do I stifle within myself the yearning to reach out beyond myself for permanence—immortality if you prefer—which I can still define as "reaching towards God." Even here, I am prepared to do those "commandments" which aid me in my halting attempts to reach out beyond myself. The disciplined acts of religious commitment free my mind to search for the meaning of life in this post-Holocaust world which I now inhabit.

Admittedly, these six criteria for the observance of any and all "commandments" are subjective. But honestly recognized subjectivity is all that I have in the light of what transpired more than four decades ago. *The reality of my world is that there is no longer any authority structure, other than that to which I would willingly subject myself, that has any authority over me.* Nor can I honestly compel anyone else to observe those "commandments." I can only try and persuade those whom I am privileged to teach that there exists one *possible* way for individual persons or a family to make sense of its world, to affirm positively his/her/their Jewish selves.

Admittedly, these six criteria are selective in the sense that I—or anyone else—select from that ever-growing body of Jewish resource literature which includes the various categories of "commandments" those which give meaning to life. Thus, the only *required* "commandment" is that of study. Since I cannot command observance, the responsibility falls directly upon the shoulders of the individual to decide for oneself those "commandments" which one would willingly choose to observe. Such a mature and responsible recognition of the freedom to be and to do in this post-Holocaust world *requires* an equally mature commitment to study those same resources in order to make meaningful decisions. To refuse to do and to refuse to study is not Jewish freedom but Jewish stupidity; it is to reduce being Jewish to biology. And that notion the Nazis themselves carried to its logical and horrifying conclusion.

The time for Jewish guilt is long past. I no longer feel guilty if I do not fully observe the dietary system, if I no longer wear a *kippah* or *yarmulke* when I pray, if I take my family in the car to a picnic or the zoo on the Sabbath. I feel good about those "commandments" which I now choose to observe in a world which destroyed forever any compulsive notion to observe. In so doing, I proudly affirm my place among the Jewish People and my willingness and determination to continue to work for the physical survival of the Jewish People and the spiritual survival of those who proudly wish to call themselves Jews. And I am defiant enough to reject any attempt by anyone else to superimpose any definitions upon me as to what constitutes Jewishness or Jewish identity and to couple such definitions with external authority. The caustic query, "Who died and made you God?" has, for me, been answered by the deaths of the Six Million. Their very deaths have freed me from the constraints of the past and forced me to confront both the present and the future honestly by confronting reality "face to face." This I now choose to do to the best of my ability.

A Response to the Critiques

[*Editor's Note*: In the Summer 1988 issue of *JUDAISM*, we published a paper by Rabbi Steven L. Jacobs entitled, "(If) There is No 'Commander'? . . . There are No 'Commandments!'!" Upon its appear-

Reprinted from *JUDAISM: A Quarterly Journal of Jewish Thought* 38, no. 2 (Spring 1989): 245, 249-252. Permission granted.

ance, it elicited a strong reaction from many readers, some of whose replies (occasionally abbreviated) are reprinted in this issue. They are followed by a final statement by Rabbi Jacobs. (Robert Gordis)]

To the Editors of Judaism:

Colleagues (Rabbi Herbert) Rose (Boulder, Colorado) and (Rabbi Samuel) Weingart (West Lafayette, Indiana) honor me by taking seriously the position articulated and advanced by me in the Summer, 1988, issue of *JUDAISM*, i.e., that, in light of the *Shoah*, the only *mitzvah*, if, indeed, it is even appropriate to use that term, is that of *study* to deepen one's knowledge of what it means to be a Jew in order to make conscious, and, ultimately, subjective decisions about the kind of Jew one wishes to be; and that Jewish behavior must now posit a different rationale for action, Jewish doing, for the Jew who wishes positively to affirm his or her Jewish self and identity in a world where the historically traditional notion of Divine authority is no longer applicable. I, likewise, suggested six criteria. Nevertheless, neither Rose nor Weingart, however, address the central issue of this paper—Whether a child of a survivor can affirm Jewish behavior according to *any* historically traditional understanding?—or the larger question—Whether anyone can affirm Jewish behavior according to traditional understandings of God in light of the *Shoah*? Ironically, perhaps, but certainly most interestingly, both Rose and Weingart are representatives of a nonhalakhic movement (i.e., Reform Judaism) whose entire authority structure is subjective at best, and, therefore, extremely problematic when it comes to such core notions as *mitzvah* as commanded act of God, God as the *Mitzaveh* or Commander, and the individual Jew as the *mitzuveh* or the commanded respondent for such behaviors.

Turning directly to Rabbi Rose's concerns, my criticism of historically traditional Judaism and its understanding of God as *Mitzaveh* is not to "strike at the very foundation of the Jewish enterprise," but, rather, to acknowledge that, for *this* child of a survivor, those answers are no longer satisfactory for one who wishes to affirm his Jewish self positively and take his place within the family of the Jewish People. Appeals, therefore, to those survivors who neither lost their faith nor saw it diminished will not now suffice; even Reeve Robert Brenner, in his book *The Faith and Doubt of Holocaust Survivors*,[1] acknowledges that there were, also, those who saw their faith destroyed or diminished. My concern, religiously, is with the Second Generation, the "inheritors" of this awesome and awful historical legacy. How do *we* now make our way religiously? And what about those of us who cannot "pray as our grandparents—pious Jews murdered by the Nazis before our birth—prayed?" Is there no place for us in the world of religious Jews because we cannot affirm that which those who "believe in a personal God, the Bible, and Rabbinic Judaism" do?

"From a philosophical point of view," to quote Rabbi Rose, the question we must ask is whether or not the Holocaust is *unique* in the annals of Jewish history . . . and, therefore, is an event which demands unique responses on the part of our Jewish People in all areas where it chooses to act—including the religious. Alan Rosenberg has already addressed most succinctly this question of "uniqueness" and stressed "four kinds of evidence:"

> . . . the simple fact of the size and scope of the destruction . . . the means employed in the Holocaust . . . the varied physical and psychological qualities used to reduce the intended victims to their barest physical qualities as "objects" . . . the vast and determined attempts by the Nazis to transform the victims into the image that the Nazis had of them. (page 156)[2]

As an historian, I would, also, argue that the Holocaust was unique in the evolution of its anti-Semitism from pre-Christian notions of social and cultural anti-Semitism through Christian religious and theological anti-Semitism through post-Christian notions of political anti-Semitism to the Nazis' exploitation of "biological" anti-Semitism. Not what we did, how we behaved, how we practiced our faith and its rituals and ceremonials were at issue, but what we were was at the root of all that afflicted the Western world. "Jewishness" was a physical component of the individual, part of our very life's blood, and, thus, could no more be changed than could amputation of limb render the individual a whole human being. "Race mixing" between Jew and Aryan, according to the Nazis, had to result in an inferiorization and mongrelization of the Aryan race; there was simply no other way to perceive that negative relationship.

Philosphically and historically, therefore, this unique evil may be said to be a transformational event, one which calls forth responses, both positive and negative, because the reality of our world has now changed dramatically from what it was previously, whether we like it or not. I, too, do not wish to ignore Jewish history, but previously comforting answers to past tragedies do not address the singular uniqueness of the Holocaust for some among us, especially when appeal is made in historically traditional terms.

(Parenthetically, therefore, appeals to God's commitment to human freedom will pale into insignificance when contrasted with the Torah's position of a God responsible for liberating us from the hell of Egyptian slavery, who heard our plaintive cry in that land and responded to it, but, seemingly, failed to do so—or, perhaps, more frighteningly, chose not to do so—in the hell of modern Europe. Does such a God not lose credibility to command the children and grandchildren of martyred loved ones?)

Like Rabbi Rose, I, too, am extremely uncomfortable with making the Holocaust a paradigmatic foundation for positive Jewish action and belief. But my own faith in the continuous resilience of our Jewish People also impels me to accept an understanding that even such a powerful and potent negative event, which calls forth a profound reexamination of that which is sacred to our continued survival, will result in blessing to us . . .

Lastly, I have, in no way, "cut the guts out of historic Judaism and left us with a ghostly apparition." I have suggested that what is now needed in our contemporary post-Holocaust Jewish world is a rethinking of the rationale for Jewish doing and Jewish belief. There are other sources and reasons to affirm both (e.g., history and tradition, to cite two), but appeals to a Divine Commander, for some among us, will not be one of them.[3] My faith in our Jewish People is strengthened and renewed by our historical experience, specifically, the creation of Israel itself, the result of many motivations, literally the phoenix arising out of the ashes of the Holocaust. I, also, demand, therefore, a *different* understanding of God and God's relationship to humanity, particularly the Jewish People, so that I, too, may be included in our future.

Rabbi Weingart, in turn, raises similar, but, ultimately, different concerns: He is, however, far too cavalier in his dismissal of me and my own understanding of "limited theism." In my own evolution of God's as *Borei Olam*, that God choose, for reasons which we do not fully comprehend, to "withdraw into itself" and create our world, one of possibility and potential. That act of withdrawal, however, saw at that very same moment the construction of an impenetrable barrier between God and the human community. God's commitment to this act of creation, therefore, was, ultimately, to surrender any notion of interaction and intervention into the affairs of humanity. The *Shoah*, like the creation of the State of Israel itself, *l'havdil*, is the result of human enterprise, calling forth the potential inherent in the human person. Prayer, therefore, as appeals for Divine intervention, must be regarded, historically and ultimately, as futile gestures. God is not to be blamed either for the orchestration of the *Shoah* or for the failure or refusal to act: the *Shoah*, like all human activity subsequent to the initial act of creation, is the result of human doing. The goal of prayer, then, is to give thanks for creation; the goal of human activity is to work towards the eradication of evil which impedes the drive towards harmony with the universe.

As to why I have, at least initially, chosen to address this concept of *Mitzaveh-mitzvot-mitzuvim*, I regard its evolution as central to a historically traditional notion of Judaism, one which is no longer applicable to Jews in light of the *Shoah*. Whether it was, in fact, a correct understanding of the historical relationship between God and the Jewish People is, for me, highly doubtful; the only certainty which I am prepared to affirm is that, prior to the *Shoah*, this understanding did sustain our People in times of trauma and enabled us to overcome tragedy and move forward. To regard that understanding as still applicable is highly problematic, at best, and no longer comforting at worst.

I have also chosen to address a rationale for the continued affirmation of Jewish doing because I am, also, convinced that our continued survival as Jews in this world will be dependent upon how we act—in response to our own self-perceptions and in response to both our friends and our enemies—and, that while anti-Semitism continues to rear its ugly head, we must concretely, through our actions, combat the Nazi notion of Judaism as biological phenomenon. Religiously, the *kesher*, the bond, that we Jews will make with each other must now be based on a solid understanding that we act as Jews because we choose to act as Jews, drawing upon the collective insights and literature of all previous generations of Jews. Appeals to God to ensure our future survival in light of the *Shoah* may prove comforting and sustaining to some; it will not prove so to all.

I would contend, as would Rabbi Weingart, that my position necessitates a rethinking of the covenantal relationship between God and the Jewish People. The contractual understanding of our willingness to affirm certain behaviors in exchange for Divine protection is precisely what must be rethought in light of the *Shoah*. Theologically, would we not, conversely, come perilously close to a rationale for the *Shoah* as the result of Jewish failure to honor our historical covenantal commitments? Such a conclusion could, I believe, be derived from a Torahitic understanding of covenant, one which, I likewise believe, even the most literal among us would hesitate to affirm. [Equally problematic, however, is Irving Greenberg's "voluntary" covenant, though it does, to be sure, come closer to an honest description of present-day Jewish reality than anyone else's with which I am familiar.[4] Better, then, to think in terms of a new understanding of covenant, "a covenant of thanksgiving," whereby Jews affirm those initial acts that enabled us to come into being as singularly unique and distinctive collectivity, possessed of the potential to sustain ourselves and withstand onslaught after onslaught. By extension, we must take this concept of covenant and use it to enter into relationships with *all* other peoples to whom we can relate, for their survival as well as our own. Out of such a rethinking may very well come a new synthesis of God, Torah, and Israel.

Notes

1. New York: Macmillan Publishing Company, 1980.

2. Alan Rosenberg, "Was the Holocaust Unique? A Peculiar Question," in Isidor Wallimann and Michael N. Dobkowski, eds., *Genocide and the Modern Age: Etiology and Case Studies of Mass Death* (New York: Greenwood Press, 1987), pages 145-161; reviewed by me in *Judaica Book News*, 18, no. 2 (Spring-Summer 1988/5748): 29-33.

3. Mordecai Bar-On has already explored these distinct possibilities in a three-part analysis which appeared in the *Reconstructionist* under the title "The Commandments and the 'Commander'" (October 1977): 7-12, 31; (November 1977): 24-30; and (December 1977): 17-24. Interestingly enough, Misha Louvish translated Bar-On's lengthy essay and has himself addressed this very topic from the perspective of a secularist. See Misha Louvish, "The Problems of a Secular Jew," *The Jerusalem Post*, International Edition (15 October 1988), page 10.

4. Irving Greenberg, "Voluntary Covenant," in Steven L. Jacobs, ed., *Contemporary Jewish Religious Responses to the Shoah* (Lanham, Md.: University Press of America, 1993), pages 77-105; and "Cloud of Smoke, Pillar of Fire: Judaism, Christianity, and Modernity after the Holocaust," in Eva Fleischner, ed., *Auschwitz: Beginning of a New Era? Reflections on the Holocaust* (New York: Ktav Publishing House, 1977), pages 7-57.

Appendix II:
"Rethinking Jewish [and Christian?] Faith in Light of the Holocaust: The Response of the Child of a Survivor"

I

The Jewish People and all of contemporary humanity is, at best, but a single generation away from the nightmarish events of the Holocaust. Though the wound itself continues to fester, survivors and their offspring, as well as those only indirectly affected, continue to experience healing. Indeed, the very fact that there are offspring of those who experienced the unspeakable is, in and of itself, one measure of that healing. That this "Second Generation," the offspring of the original survivors as they are now called and now call themselves, in turn chooses to have children furthers that healing, and may very well be the loudest response to Adolf Hitler's quest for a world *Judenrein*, Jew-free.

Problematic, however, is the literature which addresses the "inheritance" of this Second Generation of victims, the children of diminished families, from the perspective of Jewish faith, belief, and practice.[1] The concerns of many writers are not with the faith of this Second Generation and issues and concerns related to that faith, but, rather, with the psychological health and well-being of these children of survivors. The works of Bergmann and Jucovy, Luel and Marcus, Eitinger and Krell, and Dimsdale all address religious issues

Reprinted from *The New Collegian* [of Samford University, a Baptist institution of higher learning, Birmingham, Alabama] 3, no. 1 (1990): 13-17. Permission Granted. Although thoroughly revised, the genesis of this essay was a presentation to the Third Annual Conference on Spirituality of the Atlanta Reform Jewish Synagogue Council on Sunday, 21 September 1986, under the theme "Reform Jews in Search of God: The *Mitzvot*—Law or Lore?" That presentation was itself published as the previous appendix.

when writing about the Second Generation, but they do so within the framework of psychological and psychoanalytic thought.[2] Significant, too, both the *Journal of Contemporary Psychotherapy*[3] and *Journal of Psychology and Judaism*[4] devoted "special issues" to the survivors and their children, but, again, used a frame of reference other than the religious. Helen Epstein's *Children of the Holocaust: Conversations with Sons and Daughters of Survivors* lets the Second Generation speak in its own words out of its own pathos.[5] Powerfully expressed as the concerns of the children are, here, too, it is not the religiously affirmative, negated or problematic which ties the stories together, but human and family concerns. Lastly, Reeve Robert Brenner's *The Faith and Doubt of Holocaust Survivors*, while proving a true "window of insight" into the religious thinking of his population sample of predominantly Israeli survivors, says almost nothing about their children.[6]

Then, too, those Jewish writers who have directly confronted the Holocaust and its religious and theological implications—Eliezer Berkovits, Arthur Cohen, Emil Fackenheim, Irving Greenberg, Bernard Maza, and, of course, Richard L. Rubenstein—have profoundly and eloquently presented their thoughts to the worldwide Jewish community.[7] But, like the "psychological school," they have not directly extended their thinking to the impact of the legacy of the Holocaust upon the very generation who have now grown to maturity as adults, marriage partners, and parents, deeply affected by the experiences of their parents, still connected to and committed to the Jewish people and faith, but no longer either comfortable with or contented with the historically traditional responses of Judaism. That Christian writers on the Holocaust have not addressed this particular audience should come as no surprise: The foci of their concerns have been twofold: (1) to build a bridge of reconciliation with the Jewish people, and (2) to make their own Christian communities more fully aware of the religious and philosophical, not to mention historical, implications of the Holocaust.[8]

What follows, then, is a *preliminary* investigation and exploration of those topic areas central to the Jewish faith experience by one child of a survivor, now deceased, with a primary concern being that of the concept of the "Commander-commandment" continuum, a rethinking of the whole notion of *mitzvot* or religiously commanded obligation Jewishly understood. Only indirectly will the implications of this journey for contemporary Christianity be addressed.

II

1. Both the Bible and postbiblical or Rabbinic Judaism (not to men-
    tion Christianity) present their understanding of Deity as the
    God-who-acts-in-history, whose caring and concern for Jews
    was ultimately expressed at Sinai (and through Jesus the Christ
    for Christians at Calvary), for reasons largely unknown to His
    human children. No longer acceptable or comforting, when jux-
    taposed to the Holocaust, is the *midrashic* (i.e., interpretive)
    understanding of a Deity, who, sadly, went with His children
    into exile in Egypt and rejoiced, gladly, with them when they
    celebrated their liberation from slavery and bondage. No amount
    of rationalization can overcome the enormity of the loss of 6
    million (over 150 in my case) by asserting that Providence pre-
    vented the number from escalating higher. If truth now be told:
    not only did 6 million of our Jewish brothers and sisters die at
    Auschwitz, as well as 5 million non-Jews, but the historically
    traditional notion of God also died, for some among us, in the
    concentration camps which puncture the landscape of Europe.

    What is now demanded in the realm of theological
    integrity is a notion of Deity compatible with the reality of radi-
    cal evil at work and at play in our world, a notion which, also,
    admits of human freedom for good or evil without fruitless
    appeals to a Deity who "chose" not to act because He or She
    could not act. To continue to affirm the historically traditional
    notions of faith in God as presented by both Biblical and
    Rabbinic traditions (as well as Christianity) is to ignore the
    Holocaust with all of its uniqueness and to ignore those who,
    like myself, continue to feel the pain of family loss, yet want to
    remain committed to Jewish survival, not because Deity wills it,
    but because without even this battered community, we are cut
    off from this most fragile of moorings.

2. Such a different understanding of Deity is, however, contingent
    upon accepting the Holocaust as a unique and radical depar-
    ture from the "normative" development and evolution of Jewish
    and world history. While the debate still rages in both schol-
    arly[9] and religious[10] circles, for the child of survivors, armed
    with even a minimal knowledge of Jewish history and tragedy,
    the Holocaust is literally "something else," and must be so
    regarded or ignored. How else to understand the shift from pre-

Christian manifestations of antisemitism to and through theological and religious antisemitism to the "modern" notion of biological antisemitism from which no Jew could escape, including the members of one's own family? How else to understand the very modernity of the Holocaust as the marriage of bureaucratic excellence and technological perfection which perceived *Die Endlosung*, the "Final Solution," within the realm of human possibilities? How else to confront the pain of loss and, even haltingly, begin to make some sense of it?

3. Such an understanding is, likewise, contingent upon accepting a notion of God as other than historically and traditionally presented by both Judaism and Christianity. A possible source of Divine affirmation, to the degree to which such affirmation is either desired or acknowledged as desired, lies in the concept of "limited Deity" who could neither choose nor reject action during the dark years of 1933(39)-1945, who could not have responded to those humanly created and crafted processes of destruction even if He or She had wanted to do so. Notions of omniscience and omnipotence quickly fall by the wayside; the alternative possibilities are a Deity who was ignorant of the designs of His or Her German children and their European cousins and impotent to act even when He or She learned of their plans, or a limited Deity whose own nonknowledge and limited power precluded both foreknowledge and interference. The very technology of Nazism forever shattered the easy appeal to a Deity who will, somehow, curb the limits of human intellect and action for evil or good, and, in the future, prevent a repetition or recurrence of the Holocaust. If anything, the reverse is now possible: Having let the genie of destructive forces out of the bottle of human ignorance, our best hope for survival lies not in the heavens, but in our ability to educate the next generation to evince the same intellectual expertise to creative measures as has thus far been evidenced to destructive measures.

4. Of necessity, the notion of *Brith* or Covenant must now be redefined. A violated but never abrogated Biblical understanding of Covenant only makes sense in relation to the God-who-acts-in-history. Covenant with Deity whereby both Divine and human partners agree to certain stipulations in order to maintain harmony and equilibrium is no longer logical nor desirable outside of such historically traditional ways of thinking. Greenberg's

"Voluntary Covenant" becomes an option only for those who wish to enter into it, as does its opposite, a rejection of the entire enterprise.[11] We can no longer trust in our supposed covenantal relationship with God to keep the enemy from crouching at our door. Nor could Deity, however understood, trust us not to act in ways that would prove either a one-time or perpetual violation of sacred trusts regarding the living things of our planet.

If we are now to enter into religiously sensitized and renewed and renewable covenants, they must now be with each other, as individuals, as communities, as nation-states. Having now actualized the potential to destroy larger and larger groups, having now been the recipients of such destruction, we must guard against repetition by our continual willingness to engage in dialogue despite our differences, and even with those whose value systems we fundamentally reject. Russians and Americans, Jews and Christians, Jews and Jews, Jews and Arabs, Jews and Germans, Christians and Christians must, in fact, enter into "covenants of dialogue." Appeals to Deity will not make such conversations possible, nor will appeals to historical relationships or nonrelationships. Only our direct appeals to each other will.

5. Prayer, too, now stands in need of rethinking. Appeals to Deity to correct present situations or to dramatically alter future possibilities have now proven themselves of no avail. Having realized no response from On High to words spoken in earnestness and fervor during the long dark night of Nazisms' all-too-successful reign of terror, to now expect God to respond on a less frightful level, to less critical pleas, is theological absurdity. Unless, of course, one is prepared to accept a God only able to deal with the inconsequential rather than the consequential, equally a theological absurdity. Prayer will now have to become an internal plea for recognition that the universe does manifest certain harmonies if we are but receptive to them; that creation allows more possibilities for human growth than does destruction; that aesthetic pleasure of our world enhances our pleasure at being part of it; that the prayerfully poetic words of our predecessors, now reinterpreted, likewise, increases the shared yearnings of all humankind for peace; that the disciplined gatherings of like-minded groups in celebration and in sorrow can help energize us to confront the challenges of our own day;

and, lastly, and most importantly, that we need not suspend our intellect nor deny historical realities, most particularly the Holocaust, when we engage in prayer.

6.   At the heart of the Jewish experience is the notion of *mitzvah* or "commandment" as obligated act in response to the "call" of the *Mitzaveh* or "Commander." Having tentatively and painfully rethought such notions of God, Covenant, and Prayer, to continue to maintain such an historically traditional notion of *mitzvah* not only begs the question, but negates the historical realities of the Holocaust itself. The classical understanding of *mitzvah* is itself an affirmation of a relationship no longer extent. "God calls, we respond through *mitzvot*, and God, in turn, responds to us" is no longer creditable. Fackenheim's "commanding voice at Auschwitz," heard only by those already listening, will not be heard by those already sensitized or not so sensitized to their Jewish (and Christian?) responsibilities because of the events of the Holocaust. Besides, even Fackenheim would not have the temerity to maintain that this voice is the Divine Voice of talmudic tradition which seemingly spoke to the rabbis in the ancient academies so very long ago. Thus, the notion of *mitzvah* as the religiously commanded act of Deity to creation, imposed upon the Jewish people by an historically bound and committed Authority and authority structure, is, truly, yet another victim of the Holocaust.

7.   In light of the Holocaust, then, having now, sadly, rejected the understanding of God as *Mitzaveh*, "Commander," the question remains: "What criteria or standards can or do we use to incorporate into our lives Jewish (and Christian) behavior, both ritual-ceremonial and ethical-moral, even if we no longer regard them as "commandments?" If we are honest and truthful with ourselves, there are six.
      a.   *Intellectual*: One should be willing to incorporate into one's Jewish (and Christian) behavior acts which do not offend against one's intellectual understanding of reality, and, also, appeal to an awareness of order and precision in the universe of which one is a part. It is not that one is bound to them by some external Presence or Force; it is, rather, than one chooses to bind oneself to those specifically Jewish (and Christian) acts and behaviors which "make sense." The rhythmic celebration of the Sabbath is, perhaps, the pre-

mier example by which one can intellectually bind oneself to the Jewish people religiously.

b. *Aesthetic*: Too, there are those Jewish (and Christian) acts which provide one with a sense of aesthetic pleasure. Visually, aurally, orally, tactilely, and, yes, even through a sense of smell. That sense of Jewish (and Christian) "pleasure," therefore, may very well be a sufficient reason for the doing of certain acts or behaviors for that reason alone. The Scrolls of the Torah garbed in white for the High Holy Days, the voice of the cantor, the waving of the palm branch at *Sukkot*, the savoring of the spices marking the end of the Sabbath come readily to mind.

c. *Emotional*: For the child of survivors who wishes to affirm his or her place within the totality of the Jewish people subsequent to the Holocaust by involvement in various Jewish and non-Jewish agencies, institutions, and organizations, such involvements can meet emotional needs and further result in additional Jewish acts and behaviors. Involvement specifically in the synagogue, as the *primary* institution of Jewish religious life, however, can both raise the issues questioned at this essay's beginning, and, at the same time, provide the warm, nurturing environment where they can be explored safely and without pressure. Such would, also, obviously be applicable to Christianity.

d. *Physical*: There are, likewise, those Jewish (and Christian) acts and behaviors which have a strong physical component to their doing, and evoke Jewishly affirming responses. The "Covenant of circumcision" of one's own or one's family's or friend's sons, holding aloft the Torah Scrolls on the appropriate festival occasions, even fasting on the Day of Atonement, address uniquely the physical part of one's being and further connect one with the Jewish community and Jewish people.

e. *Psychological*: Closely akin to the emotional, participation in the life-cycle and festival-cycle of the Jewish people may express a certain validity to the individual child of survivors in light of the Holocaust, and may yet meet important psychological needs, primarily that of loneliness versus nonloneliness.

f. *Spiritual*: Lastly, rejection of the historically traditional notion of God because of its failure to address the reality of the Holocaust does not, in and of itself, remove one from

involvement in the Jewish (and Christian) religious enterprise. Nor does a rethinking and restructuring of the understanding of the Jewish (and Christian) religious acts and
behaviors away from the time-honored and time-understood
idea of "commandment" called forth by the "Commander"
negate one's involvement in the Jewish (and Christian) religious tradition. That sense of awe and wonder at life and the
universe, that yearning to reach out beyond for a sense of
permanence, are no less real to one whose inherited legacy
is as the child of survivors than one who is not so described.
The disciplined acts of religious commitment enable one to
reach out beyond oneself, both horizontally towards community and vertically towards the future, and best enable
one to be free to search and explore the meaning of life in
this post-Holocaust and post-Auschwitz world.

8.   Admittedly, these six criteria by which to evaluate Jewish (and
Christian) noncommanded acts and behaviors are subjective. But
honestly recognized subjectivity is all that remains in light of what
transpired better than four decades ago. The reality of our world is
that, because of the Holocaust, there is no longer any religious
authority structure other than that to which one willingly and affirmatively commits oneself. Compulsion, either Divine or human,
has become morally problematic and will forever remain so.

9.   Likewise, these six criteria are selective in that any Jew (or
Christian) is now free to select from the ever-growing body of
Jewish (or Christian) resource literature that which gives Jewish
(or Christian) meaning to one's life. Thus, there is now only
one required "commandment" or "obligation:" that of study.
The responsibility now falls directly upon the shoulders of the
individual Jew (or Christian) to decide for oneself those Jewish
(or Christian) "obligations" which one would willingly choose to
observe. Such a mature and responsible recognition of the freedom to be and to do in this post-Holocaust world Jewishly (and
Christianly?) requires an equally mature commitment to study
those same resources in order to make Jewishly (and Christianly)
meaningful decisions. To refuse to do so and to refuse to study
in order to do so now becomes the height of irresponsibility.

10.   Celebration and commemoration both life-cycle and festival-cycle
events will have to be rethought, not so much for the manner in

which they are celebrated, but for the rationale behind their celebration. No more can this holiday or that life-cycle event be
celebrated or sanctified for the historically-traditional reasons
previously supplied. Though the actual practices themselves may
not vary one iota from previous patterns of behavior, the "whys"
and "wherefores," in light of the Holocaust, now demand a
degree of intellectual consistency, coupled with theological
integrity, not necessarily required in Judaism's (or Christianity's)
long past. No more can Passover, for example, be viewed as
God's liberation of the Jewish people from slavery and bondage
in Egypt, when the slavery and bondage of Nazi Germany
resulted in the death and degradation of so many. No longer can
the "covenant of circumcision" of an 8-day-old Jewish male be
understood as entering into covenant directly with God, when
those already so committed to that covenant realized its impotence throughout Nazi-occupied Europe, and transmitted such,
ofttimes not even in words, but in feelings and expressions to the
Second Generation. New words are needed to address new realities; if not new words, then new interpretations of old words,
not for all, but certainly for those among us for whom the old
ways can no longer be maintained or resurrected.[12]

11.   Though it would obviously be somewhat presumptuous to elab-
      orate those categories central to the Christian religious experi-
      ence which now need to be rethought after the Holocaust, the
      following three areas do suggest themselves to this writer. The
      working out of other categories, as well as the future elaboration
      of those suggested above and below, are better left to Christian
      philosophers and theologians, better equipped by virtue of their
      own training, to grapple with their implications.
      a.   The whole notion of the redeeming Christ in an unre-
           deemed world which would countenance a Holocaust,
      b.   The "mission" of the Church in relationship to the Jewish
           people in the post-Auschwitz world, and
      c.   The "proper" relationship between Judaism and
           Christianity, between Jews and Christians, in the aftermath
           of the Second World War.

III

The time for Jewish (and Christian) guilt is long past. To include
among us only those who are now willing to maintain past structures

is equally as pernicious as excluding those who no longer wish to do so. What is of relevance are those Jews (and Christians) who, freely, are willing to make positively affirmative commitments, who are willing to practice those forms of historically traditional behaviors which they themselves find meaningful, both individually and collectively, as well as those who do not choose to do so. The "bottom line" must be the willingness to make these commitments and not the standards by which any subgroup of Jews (or Christians) chooses to evaluate its own members. To presume guilt towards those who no longer think and act in accord with the ways of the past is to deny both the present and the future. The focus must be inclusive rather than exclusive if our world is to maintain any sense of equilibrium given the contemporary pressures with which it is currently confronted, and, in the process, make room for the Jewish children of Holocaust survivors and their descendants.

The caustic query, "Who died and made you God?"has been answered for some among us by the deaths of the 6 million; their deaths have forced some among us to confront both the restraints of the past and a future no longer bound by those constraints. Out of such a confrontation may very well come a new synthesis for Jews of God, Torah, and Israel, and a new relationship between Jews and Christians.

Notes

1. That the issue of "faith after the Holocaust" has not been adequately addressed by either the Jewish or Christian faith-communities is, in part, the substance of my own essay "Judaism and Christianity After Auschwitz" in Steven L. Jacobs, ed., *Contemporary Jewish Religious Responses to the Shoah* (Lanham, Md.: University Press of America, 1993), pages 1-23.

2. [For a list of these writers' works, see "Notes and Bibliography."]

3. Special Issue: Holocaust Survivors: Psychological and Social Sequelae, 2, no. 1 (Spring-Summer 1980).

4. Special Issue: Holocaust Aftermath: Continuing Impact on the Generations, 6, no. 1, (Fall-Winter 1981).

5. New York: G. P. Putnam's Sons, 1979.

6. New York: The Free Press, 1980.

7. [For a list of the works of these writers, see "Notes and Bibliography."]

8. [For a list of the works of some of these writers, see "Notes and Bibliography."]

9. See, for example, Yehuda Bauer, "Against Mystification: The Holocaust as Historical Perspective," in *The Holocaust in Historical Perspective* (London: Sheldon Press, 1978), pages 30-49; Henry L. Feingold, "Determining the Uniqueness of the Holocaust: The Factor of Historical Value?" *Shoah*, 2 (Spring 1981): 3-11, 30; Alan Rosenberg, "Was the Holocaust Unique? A Peculiar Question," in Isidor Wallimann and Michael N. Dobkowski, eds., *Genocide and the Modern Age: Etiology and Case Studies of Mass Death* (New York: Greenwood Press, 1987), pages 145-161.

10. See, for example, the report of the speech by British chief rabbi Sir Immanuel Jakobovitz, "Religious Responses to the Holocaust: Retrospect and Prospect" to the B'nai B'rith in Jerusalem, entitled "The Holocaust Was Not Unique," in *The Jerusalem Post*, International Edition (December 1977), page 6. According to reporter Haim Shapiro, in that same speech, Jakobovitz also "expressed his own conviction that the State of Israel would not have come into being had it not been for this tragedy." See, also, David W. Weiss, "After the Holocaust, Another Covenant?" *Sh'ma: A Journal of Jewish Responsibility* 14, no. 272 (April 13, 1984): 89-91. Martin A. Cohen, in "The Mission of Israel After Auschwitz," also presents a brief survey of traditional Jewish thinkers who reject the notion of uniqueness with regard to the Holocaust in Helga Croner and Leon Kleinicki, eds., *Issues in the Jewish-Christian Dialogue: Jewish Perspectives on Covenant, Mission and Witness* (New York: Paulist Press, 1979), pages 157-181.

11. Irving Greenberg, "Voluntary Covenant," in Steven L. Jacobs, ed., *Contemporary Jewish Religious Responses to the Shoah* (Lanham, Md.: University Press of America, 1993), pages 77-105.

12. For a relatively recent attempt at wrestling with the implications of the Holocaust, see Robert Gordis, "A Cruel God or None: The Challenge of the Holocaust," in his *Judaic Ethics for a Lawless World* (New York: The Jewish Theological Seminary of America, 1986), pages 79-93. Gordis's five biblical insights are (1) the glory of life and the goodness of God, (2) man's right and duty to confront evil in the world, (3) the core of mystery in evil, (4) man's freedom, and (5) the interdependence of mankind are worthy of fuller exploration in relation to the Holocaust, but Gordis' focus is not on that with which this essay is primarily concerned, that of rethinking the "categories" central to the Jewish religious enterprise in light of the Holocaust.

Notes and Bibliography

"Introduction: Why? The Genesis of My Own Thinking"

For a further look at my own family, see my recently published account of the letters of my grandparents, Leo and Ella Jacob, murdered by the Nazis in late 1941 or early 1942, entitled "Letters from Zerbst," in G. Jan Colijn and Marcia S. Littell, eds., *The Netherlands and Nazi Genocide: Papers of the Twenty-First Annual Scholars Conference* (Lewiston, N.Y.: Edwin Mellen Press, 1992), pages 505-518.

Among the "Second Generation" books that address us as children of our survivors, our parents, and our own particular concerns and dilemmas are the following: Helen Epstein, *Children of the Holocaust: Conversations with Sons and Daughters of Survivors* (New York: G. P. Putnam's Sons, 1979); Aaron Hass, *In the Shadow of the Holocaust: The Second Generation* (Ithaca, N.Y.: Cornell University Press, 1990); Peter Sichrovsky, *Strangers in Their Own Land: Young Jews in Germany and Austria Today* tran. Jean Steinberg (New York: Basic Books, 1986); and "The Holocaust: Our Generation Looks Back," *Response: A Contemporary Jewish Review*, 9, no. 1 (Spring 1975).

Also addressing the Second Generation, but not limited to it, from the "psychological" perspective are Martin S. Bergman and Milton E. Jucovy, eds., *Generations of the Holocaust* (New York, Basic Books, 1982); Joel E. Dimsdale, ed., *Survivors, Victims, and Perpetrators: Essays on the Holocaust* (Washington, D.C.: Hemisphere Publishing Corporation, 1980); Leo Eitinger and Robert Krell, *The Psychological and Medical Effects of Concentration Camps and Related Persecutions on Survivors of the Holocaust: A Research Bibliography* (Vancouver: University of British Columbia Press, 1985); Steven A. Luel and Paul Marcus, *Psychoanalytic Reflections on the Holocaust: Selected Essays* (New York: Ktav Publishing House, 1984); as well as two "special issues" of *Journal of Contemporary Psychology*, 11, no. 1 (Spring-Summer 1980) "Holocaust Survivors: Psychological and Social Sequelae"; *Journal of Psychology and Judaism*, 6, no. 1, (Fall-Winter 1981) "Holocaust Aftermath: Continuing Impact on the Generations."

Recently, four books have appeared that deal with the "Other Second Generation," the children of the Nazi perpetrators, and are equally important for the necessary work of healing and reconciliation: Daniel Bar-On, *Legacy of Silence: Encounters with Children of the Third Reich* (Cambridge, Mass.: Harvard University Press, 1989); Niklas Frank, *In the Shadow of the Third Reich*, trans. Arthur S. Weinsinger and Carole Clew-Hoey (New York: Alfred A. Knopf, 1991); Gerald L. Posner, *Hitler's Children: Sons and Daughters of*

Leaders of the Third Reich Talk About Themselves and Their Fathers (New York: Random House, 1991); Peter Sichrovsky, *Born Guilty: Children of Nazi Families*, trans. Jean Steinberg (New York: Basic Books, 1988).

Among those books and articles by *Jewish* scholars and theologians attempting to understand and interpret the *Shoah* that have had an enormous impact on my own thinking and development have been the following: Eliezer Berkovits, *Faith After the Holocaust* (New York: Ktav Publishing House, 1973); Arthur Cohen, *The Tremendum: A Theological Interpretation of the Holocaust* (New York: Crossroads Publishing Company, 1981); Emil Fackenheim, *The Jewish Return into History: Reflections in the Age of Auschwitz and a New Jerusalem* (New York: Schocken Books, 1978); Irving Greenberg, "Cloud of Smoke, Pillar of Fire: Judaism, Christianity, and Modernity After the Holocaust," in Eva Fleischner, ed., *Auschwitz: Beginning of a New Era? Reflections on the Holocaust* (New York, Ktav Publishing House, 1976); Bernard Maza, *With Fury Poured out: A Torah Perspective on the Holocaust* (New York, Ktav Publshing House, 1986); and Richard L. Rubenstein, *After Auschwitz: Radical Theology and Contemporary Judaism* (Indianapolis, Bobbs-Merrill Company, 1966). Additional works by all of these authors have also been studied and contemplated.

Books and articles by *Christian* scholars, thinkers, and theologians that have been important to me include the following: Harry James Cargas, *A Christian Response to the Holocaust* (Denver: Stonehenge Books, 1981) and idem., ed., *When God and Man Failed: Non-Jewish Views of the Holocaust* (New York: Macmillan Company, 1981); Alan Ecclestone, *Night Sky of the Lord* (New York: Schocken Books, 1983); Alice Lyons Eckardt, "Post-Holocaust Theology: A Journey out of the Kingdom of Night," *Holocaust and Genocide Studies*, 1, no. 2 (1986): 229-240; Alice Lyons Eckardt and A. Roy Eckardt, *Elder and Younger Brothers: The Encounter of Jews and Christians* (New York: Charles Scribner's Sons, 1967) and *Long Night's Journey into Day: A Revised Perspective on the Holocaust* (Detroit: Wayne State University Press and Oxford: Oxford University Press, 1988); Michel B. McGarry, *Christology After Auschwitz* (New York: Paulist Press, 1977); Franklin Littell, *The Crucifixion of the Jews: The Failure of Christians to Understand the Jewish Experience* (New York: Harper and Row, 1975); John Pawlikowski, "The Holocaust and Catholic Theology," *Shoah*, 2 (1980): 6ff; David A. Rausch, *A Legacy of Hatred: Why Christians Must Not Forget the Holocaust* (Chicago: Moody Institute Press, 1984); John K. Roth, *A Consuming Fire: Encounters with Elie Wiesel and the Holocaust* (Atlanta: John Knox Press, 1979); Rosemany Radford Ruether, *Faith and Fratricide: The Theological Roots of Anti-Semitism* (New York: Seabury Press, 1974); Gerard S. Sloyan, "Some Theological Implications of the Holocaust," *Interpretation*, 4 (1985).[1]

Last, in terms of the exacting nature of the work serious *Shoah* research and thinking entails, studying under the late Uriel Tal of Hebrew University during his visiting professorship at the Hebrew Union College-Jewish Institute of Religion, Cincinnati, Ohio, during my rabbinical student days, deepened my own commitment to this field of scholarship. His book *Christians and Jews in Germany: Religion, Politics, and Ideology in the Second Reich, 1870-1914* (Ithaca, N.Y.: Cornell University Press, 1975), published after my ordination, continues to serve me as a model of scholarly work.

1. The Problem with God

For me, for a proper understanding of the *Shoah* and its historical, philosophical, theological, religious, ethical, and moral implications, the first question I had to answer was that of its "uniqueness"—yes or no. Alan Rosenberg's essay, "Was the Holocaust Unique? A Peculiar Question," in Isidor Walliman and Michael N. Dobkowski, eds., *Genocide and the Modern Age: Etiology and Case Studies of Mass Death* (New York, Greenwood Press, 1987), pages 145-161, more than adequately summarizes my own thinking on this subject.

Second, a proper understanding, if such is even possible, of the *Shoah* in all of its many and varied dimensions can initially be perceived only through some of the more important "survey texts," among which I would include the following: Raul Hilberg's magisterial *The Destruction of the European Jews* (Chicago: Quadrangle Books, 1961), now expanded into a three-volume magnum opus (New York: Holmes and Meier, 1985.[2] Equally insightful is Lucy Dawidowicz's *The War Against the Jews 1933-1945* (New York: Holt, Rinehart and Winston and Philadelphia: Jewish Publication Society of America, 1975), and its companion volume *A Holocaust Reader* (New York: Behrman House, 1976).[3]

Other one-volume "survey texts" include Yehuda Bauer, *A History of the Holocaust* (New York: Franklin Watts, 1982); Martin Gilbert, *The Holocaust: A History of the Jews of Europe During the Second World War* (New York: Holt, Rinehart and Winston, 1985); Nora Levin, *The Holocaust: The Destruction of European Jewry* (New York: Thomas Y. Crowell Company, 1968); Gerald Reitlinger, *The Final Solution*, new and rev. ed. (South Brunswick, N.J.: Thomas Yoseloff, 1961); Ward Rutherford, *Genocide: The Jews of Europe 1939-1945* (New York: Ballantine Books, 1973); Gerhard Shoenberner, *The Yellow Star: The Persecution of the Jews in Europe 1933-1945*, trans. Susan Sweet (New York: Bantam Books, 1973); Leni Yahil, *The Holocaust: The Fate of European Jewry* (New York: Oxford University Press, 1990).

A fictionalized account of the *Shoah* experience, later turned into a three-part television "mini-series" shown all over the world is Gerald Green's *Holocaust* (New York: Bantam Books, 1978).

The still-definitive one-volume history of the Nazi Third Reich remains that of William L. Shirer, *The Rise and Fall of the Third Reich: A History of Nazi Germany* (Greenwich, Conn.: Fawcett Publications, 1960).

Individual testimonies and witness accounts abound in the hundreds and thousands. Two indispensable accounts of the victims are Azriel

Eisenberg's *The Lost Generation* (New York: The Pilgrim Press, 1982) and *Witness to the Holocaust* (New York: The Pilgrim Press, 1981). From the "other side" are two German accounts, now translated into English, Ernest Klee, Willi Dressen, and Volker Reiss, *"The Good Old Days:" The Holocaust as Seen by Its Perpetrators*, trans. Deborah Burnstone (New York: The Free Press, 1988); and Johannes Steinhoff, Peter Pechel, and Dennis Showalter, *Voices from the Third Reich: An Oral History* (Washington, D.C.: Regnery Gateway, 1989).

Last, an important book that combines both historical material and analytic exploration of that material is Richard L. Rubenstein and John K. Roth, *Approaches to Auschwitz: The Holocaust and Its Legacy* (Atlanta, John Knox Press, 1987).

All of the theological authors, Jewish and Christian, cited in the "Introduction" have themselves wrestled with the presence or absence of God during the *Shoah* and contributed enormously to my thinking in this area. I would, however, add two additional books: Martin Buber, *The Eclipse of God: Studies in the Relation Between Religion and Psychotherapy* (Atlantic Highlands, N.J.: Humanities Press International, 1988) and Andre Neher, *The Exile of the Word: From the Silence of the Bible to the Silence of Auschwitz* (Philadelphia, Jewish Publication Society of America, 1981).

2. Covenant: Involuntary? Voluntary? Nonexistent?

In addition to my own biblical studies during my rabbinical student days and subsequent to them, George E. Mendenhall's *The Tenth Generation: The Origins of the Biblical Tradition* (Baltimore: Johns Hopkins University Press, 1973) has also sharpened my thinking about the Covenant.

Perhaps the most "creative" exploration of this theme of Covenant after the *Shoah* is that of Irving Greenberg, "Voluntary Covenant" in my *Contemporary Jewish Religious Responses to the Shoah* (Lanham, Md.: University Press of America, 1993), pages 89-122.

3. The Crises of Prayer

Living in a "scientific age," communication-prayer with an interactive deity, as historically and traditionally understood by both Judaism and Christianity, is extremely problematic, all the more so in light of the *Shoah*. Evidence of that deity's interaction is, likewise, difficult, though I continue to be fascinated by the fact that, within the scientific community, there are those who are beginning to ask "religious" and "theological" questions. I am not at all sure, however, that enough of us in the religious-theological community are beginning to ask "scientific" questions.

A number of books suggest themselves to me as places to begin this somewhat unusual dialogue, as well as places wherein a reevaluation of the entire understanding of prayer will happen: Ian G. Barbour, *Issues in Science and Religion* (New York: Harper and Row, 1966); Jim Brooks, *Origins of Life* (Michigan: Lion Publishing Company, 1985); Fritjof Capra, *The Tao of Physics: An Exploration of the Parallels Between Modern Physics and Eastern Mysticism* (Boston: New Science Library, 1985); John L. Casti, *Paradigms Lost: Images of Man in the Mirror of Science* (New York: William Morrow and Company, 1989); Paul Davies, *The Edge of Infinity: Where the Universe Came From and How It Will End* (New York: Simon and Schuster, 1981); idem, *God and the New Physics* (New York: Simon and Schuster, 1983); idem, *Superforce: The Search for a Grand Unified Theory of Nature* (New York: Simon and Schuster, 1984); Adam Ford, *Universe: God, Science and the Human Person* (Mystic, Conn.: Twenty-Third Publications, 1987); Hans-Georg Gadamer, *Truth and Method*, 2d ed. (New York, Crossroads Publishing Company, 1987); James Gleick, *Chaos: Making a New Science* (New York: Penguin Books, 1987); George Greenstein, *Symbiotic Universe: Life and Mind in the Cosmos* (New York: William Morrow and Company, 1988); Eugene T. Mallove, *The Quickening Universe: Cosmic Evolution and Human Destiny* (New York: St. Martin's Press, 1987); David Novak and Norbert Samuelson, eds., *Creation and the End of Days: Judaism and Scientific Cosmology* (Lanham, Md.: University Press of America, 1986); Ted Peters, ed., *Cosmos as Creation: Theology and Science in Consonance* (Nashville: Abingdon Press, 1989); Rudy Rucker, *The Fourth Dimension and How to Get There* (London: Rider, 1985); Edward L. Schoen, *Religious Explanations: A Model from the Sciences* (Durham, N.C.: Duke University Press, 1985); John M. Templeton and Robert L. Herrmann, *The God Who Would Be Known: Revelations of the Divine in Contemporary Science* (New York: Harper and Row, 1989); Fred Alan Wolf, *Parallel Universe: The Search for Other Worlds* (New York: Simon and Schuster, 1988); Robert Wright, *Three Scientists and Their Gods: Looking for Meaning in an Age of Information* (New York: Times Books, 1988).

4. *Halakhah* and *Mitzvot*: Law and Commandments—
The Heart of the Matter and
5. Rethinking the Jewish Life Cycle: From Birth to Death

On the subject of *halakhah* (law), the most important and significant contemporary Orthodox understanding is that of Joseph B. Soloveitchik, *Halakhic Man*, trans. Lawrence Kaplan (Philadelphia: The Jewish Publication Society of America, 1983).

On the subject of authority in general, the following sources focused my own thinking about this topic: Richard T. DeGeorge, *The Nature and Limits of Authority* (Lawrence: University of Kansas Press, 1985); R. Baine

Harris, ed., *Authority: A Philosophical Analysis* (Tuscaloosa: University of Alabama Press, 1976); John E. Skinner, *The Meaning of Authority* (Lanham, Md.: University Press of America, 1983).

A "good" introduction to traditional Orthodox Jewish thinking on the subjects of *halakhah* (law) and *mitzvot* (commandments) and their manifestations in the life of the Jewish person are the writings of the late Rabbi Hayim Halevy Donin, two books in particular: *To Be a Jew: A Guide to Jewish Observance in Contemporary Life* (New York: Basic Books, 1972) and *To Pray as a Jew: A Guide to the Prayer Book and the Synagogue Service* (New York: Basic Books, 1980). *All* Jewish movements—Orthodox, Chassidic and non-Chassidic; Conservative; Reform; Reconstructionist; Humanist; and Secularist—publish volume after volume detailing for their adherents and for those interested in how to live Jewish lives in accord with their particularistic understandings and interpretations.

A good beginning point to an historical understanding would be E. Urbach's *The Sages: The World and Wisdom of the Rabbis of the Talmud: Their Concepts and Beliefs* (Cambridge, Mass.: Harvard University Press, 1987), particularly pages 286-400. Also, the works of both Jacob Neusner and Adin Steinsaltz, both prolific authors, open up "rabbinic thinking" in a scholarly fashion. George Horowitz, *The Spirit of Jewish Law: A Brief Account of Biblical and Rabbinical Jurisprudence with a Special Note on Jewish Law and the State of Israel* (New York: Central Book Company, 1973) remains an important overall resource.

Rethinking the historically negativized understanding of Jewish law as obstructive to a true sense of religiosity and spirituality is Roger Brooks, *The Spirit of the Ten Commandments: Shattering the Myth of Rabbinic Legalism* (New York: Harper and Row, 1990).

6. Rethinking the Jewish Festival Cycle: The Calendar in Question

In addition to the *Encyclopedia Judaica* (Jerusalem: Keter Publishing House, 1972), which provides a high-level "objective" look at each of the Jewish holidays in individual articles, the various "festival anthologies" published by the Jewish Publication Society of America, Philadelphia, edited primarily by Phillip Goodman, provide the reader with an introduction to each of the *major* Jewish holidays in all of their diversity, both historically and contemporarily: *The Rosh Hashanah Anthology* (1970); *The Yom Kippur Anthology* (1971); *The Sukkot and Simhat Torah Anthology* (1973); *The Hanukkah Anthology* (1976); *The Purim Anthology* (1964); and *The Passover Anthology* (1971). Two earlier efforts, also published by the JPSA, were Emily Solis-Cohen, Jr., *Hanukkah: The Feast of Lights* (1937) and Abraham E. Millgram, *Sabbath: The Day of Delight* (1952).[4]

7. Israel and Zionism in the Post-*Shoah* World

Books on Israel and Zionism, like books on the *Shoah*, multiply at an astonishing rate, from all of the various perspectives: historical, philosophical, theological, political, contemporary moment, critical voices, and so on. Such volumes are written by American and European Jews and Jewish and Arab Israelis, as well as Christians and Secularists. Some are popularizations, factual or fictional; others are serious literary efforts, both scholarly and journalistic. Where, then, to begin remains the question.

A good introduction to Israel is the two volumes written by Howard Morely Sachar: *A History of Israel: From the Rise of Zionism to Our Time* (New York: Alfred A. Knopf, 1979) and *From the Aftermath of the Yom Kippur War* (New York: Oxford University Press, 1987).

Equally, a good introduction to Zionism is that of Arthur Hertzberg, ed., *The Zionist Idea: A Historical Analysis and Reader* (New York: Atheneum, 1973), especially his lengthy Introduction. Additionally important studies are Shlomo Avineri, *The Making of Modern Zionism: The Intellectual Origins of the Jewish State* (London: Weidenfeld and Nicolson, 1981); Ben Halpern, *The Idea of the Jewish State* (Cambridge, Mass.: Harvard University Press, 1976); Walter Laquer, *A History of Zionism* (London: Weidenfeld and Nicolson, 1972); David Vital, *The Origins of Zionism* (Oxford: Clarendon Press, 1975).

Negatively critical assessments of contemporary Israel and Zionism are found in the writings of Christians Rosemary Radford Ruether and Herman J. Ruether, *The Wrath of Jonah: The Crisis of Religious Nationalism in the Middle East* (New York: Harper and Row, 1989) and Jews Noam Chomsky, *The Fateful Triangle: The United States, Israel and the Palestinians* (Boston: South End Press, 1983) and Marc H. Ellis, *Beyond Innocence and Redemption: Confronting the Holocaust and Israeli Power: Creating a Moral Future for the Jewish People* (New York: Harper and Row, 1990), and others, counterbalanced, perhaps, by work such as Thomas Friedman, *From Beirut to Jerusalem* (New York: Farrar, Straus and Giroux, 1989); Joan Peters, *From Time Immemorial: The Origins of the Arab-Jewish Conflict over Palestine* (New York: Harper and Row, 1984); and David Shipler, *Arab and Jew: Wounded Spirits in a Promised Land* (New York: Times Books, 1986), and others. And so the seesaw and pendulum go, swinging back and forth between supporters and detractors, defenders and attackers on both sides, Jewish and Israeli and Arab and Palestinian.[5]

Perhaps, at this critically important historical juncture, the best one can do is read anything and everything related to Israel and Zionism one can find, recognizing in the process the biases and prejudices inherent in the writing, and the complexities of the issues discussed, and then make an attempt at both assessement and understanding. What is paramount, however, is to commit oneself to work for peace throughout the Middle East, to press for an acceptance of the *reality* of the State of Israel, and an immediate resolution of the Palestinian conflict.

8. Rethinking Christianity: An Outsider's Perspective

Before addressing Christianity directly, some understanding of anti-semitism is essential in the aftermath of the *Shoah*. The following books address this painfully difficult topic: Shmuel Almog, ed., *Antisemitism Through the Ages*, trans. Nathan H. Reisner (New York: Pergamon Press, 1988); Alan T. Davies, *Anti-Semitism and the Christian Mind: The Crisis of Conscience After Auschwitz* (New York: Herder and Herder, 1969) and *Anti-Semitism and the Foundations of Christianity* (New York: Paulist Press, 1979); Edward H. Flannery, *The Anguish of the Jews: Twenty-Three Centuries of Anti-Semitism* (New York: Paulist Press, 1985); Charles Y. Glock and Rodney Stark, *Christian Beliefs and Anti-Semitism* (New York: Harper and Row, 1966); Paul E. Grosser and Edwin G. Halperin, *Anti-Semitism: The Causes and Effects of a Prejudice* (Seacaucus, N.J.: Citadel Press, 1978); Jules Isaac, *The Teaching of Contempt: Christian Roots of Anti-Semitism*, trans. Clare Huchet Bishop (New York: McGraw-Hill Book Company, 1964); Charlotte Klein, *Anti-Judaism in Christian Theology*, trans. Edward Quinn (Phildelphia: Fortress Press, 1978); Samuel Sandmel, *Anti-Semitism in the New Testament?* (Philadelphia: Fortress Press, 1978); Jean-Paul Sartre, *Anti-Semite and Jew* (New York: Schocken Books, 1965); Joshua Trachtenberg, *The Devil and the Jews: The Medieval Conception of the Jew and Its Relation to Antisemitism* (Cleveland: World Publishing Company, 1961); Clark M. Williamson, *Has God Rejected His People? Anti-Judaism in the Christian Mind* (Nashville: Abingdon Press, 1982), and others.

To, somehow, put this "dark side" of the Christian-Jewish relationship on a more even keel, close attention in the aftermath of the *Shoah* must be paid to the "Righteous Gentiles," those non-Jews, primarily Christians, who risked their own lives, often at the cost of their own deaths as well as those of their families and friends, to save Jews. Important studies include Philip Friedman, *Their Brothers' Keepers* (New York: Holocaust Library, 1978); Philip Hallie, *Lest Innocent Blood Be Shed: The Story of the Village of Le Chambon and How Goodness Happened There* (New York: Harper and Row, 1979); Samuel P. Oliner and Pearl M. Oliner, *The Altruistic Personality: Rescuers of Jews in Nazi Europe* (New York: The Free Press, 1988); Carol Rittner and Sondra Myers, eds., *The Courage to Care: Rescuers of Jews During the Holocaust* (New York: New York University Press, 1986); Nechama Tec, *When Light Pierced the Darkness: Christian Rescue of Jews in Nazi-Occupied Poland* (New York: Oxford University Press, 1986).

An interesting personal account of such experiences in light of the above is that of Samuel Oliner, *Restless Memories: Recollections of the Holocaust Years* (Berkeley, Calif.: Judah L. Magnes Museum, 1986).

Turning next to Christianity as well as Jewish-Christian relations, my own studies have included the following works: Leo Baeck, *Judaism and Christianity*, trans. Walter Kaufmann (New York: Harper and Row, 1958); Augustin Cardinal Bea, *The Church and the Jewish People* (New York: Harper and Row, 1966); David Berger, *The Jewish-Christian Debate in the High*

Middle Ages: A Critical Edition of the Nizzahon Vetus: Introduction, Translation and Commentary (Philadelphia: Jewish Publication Society of America, 1959); James H. Charlesworth, ed., *Jews and Christians: Exploring the Past, Present, and Future* (New York: Crossroads Publishing Company, 1990); Martin A. Cohen and Helga Croner, eds., *Christian Mission-Jewish Mission* (New York: Paulist Press, 1982); A Roy Eckardt, *Jews and Christians: The Contemporary Meeting* (Bloomington: Indiana University Press, 1986); Morton Scott Enslin, *Christian Beginnings*, two vols. (New York, Harper and Row, 1956); Darrelll J. Fasching, ed., *The Jewish People in Christian Preaching* (Lewiston, N.Y.: Edwin Mellen Press, 1984); Gerald Friedlander, *The Jewish Sources of the Sermon on the Mount* (New York: Ktav Publishing House, 1969); Michael Goldberg, *Jews and Christians: Getting Our Stories Straight* (Nashville: Abingdon Press, 1985); Donald A. Hagner, *The Jewish Reclamation of Jesus: An Analysis and Critique of the Modern Jewish Study of Jesus* (Grand Rapids, Mich.: Academie Books, 1984); Luther H. Harshbarger and John A. Mourant, eds., *Judaism and Christianity: Perspectives and Traditions* (Boston: Allyn and Bacon, 1968); R. Trevers Herford, *Christianity in Talmud and Midrash* (New York: Ktav Publishing House, 1903); Robert Heyer, ed., *Jewish-Christian Relations* (New York: Paulist Press, 1974); Jules Isaac, *Jesus and Israel*, trans. Clare Huchet Bishop (New York: Holt, Rinehart and Winston, 1971); Walter Jacob, *Christianity Through Jewish Eyes: The Quest for Common Ground* (Cincinnati: Hebrew Union College Press, 1974); Jacob Jocz, *The Jewish People and Jesus Christ After Auschwitz: A Study in the Controversy Between Church and Synagogue* (Grand Rapids, Mich.: Baker Book House, 1981); John Koenig, *Jews and Christians in Dialogue: New Testament Foundations* (Philadelphia: Westminster Press, 1979); Hans Kung and Walter Kasper, eds., *Christians and Jews* (New York: Seabury Press, 1975); Pinhas Lapide and Jurgen Moltmann, *Jewish Monotheism and Christian Trinitarianism: A Dialogue*, trans. Leonard Swidler (Philadelphia: Fortress Press, 1981); Pinhas Lapide and Ulrich Luz, *Jesus in Two Perspectives: A Jewish-Christian Dialogue* (Minneapolis: Augsburg Publishing House, 1985); David Novak, *Jewish-Christian Dialogue: A Jewish Justification* (New York: Oxford University Press, 1989); John T. Pawlikowski, *Christ in Light of the Jewish-Christian Dialogue* (New York: Paulist Press, 1982); Abraham J. Peck, ed., *Jews and Christians After the Holocaust* (Philadelphia: Fortress Press, 1982); Douglas Pratt and Dov Bing, eds., *Judaism and Christianity: Towards Dialogue* (Auckland, New Zealand: College Communications, 1987); Stuart Rosenberg, *The Christian Problem: A Jewish View* (New York: Hippocrene Books, 1986); E. P. Sanders et al., eds., *Jewish and Christian Self-Definition*, three vols. (Philadelphia: Fortress Press, 1980, 1981, and 1982); E. P. Sanders, *Jesus and Judaism* (Philadelphia: Fortress Press, 1985); Samuel Sandmel, *A Jewish Understanding of the New Testament* (New York: University Publishers, 1960), *Judaism and Christian Beginnings* (New York: Oxford University Press, 1968), *We Jews and Jesus* (New York: Oxford University Press, 1973); Hans Joachim Schoeps, *The Jewish-Christian Argument: A History of Theologies in Conflict*, trans. David

E. Green (New York: Holt, Rinehart and Winston, 1963); Abba Hillel Silver, *Where Judaism Differed: An Inquiry into the Distinctiveness of Judaism* (New York: Macmillan Company, 1956); Clemens Thoma, *A Christian Theology of Judaism*, trans. Helga Croner (New York: Paulist Press, 1990); Trude Weiss-Rosmarin, *Judaism and Christianity: The Differences* (New York: Jonathan David Publishers, 1968); James E. Woods, ed., *Jewish-Christian Relations in Today's World* (Waco, Texas: Baylor University Press, 1971).

An important resource for further investigation is Michael Shermis, ed., *Jewish-Christian Relations: An Annotated Bibliography and Resource Guide* (Bloomington: Indiana University Press, 1988).

Additional scholarly volumes that have furthered my understanding and appreciation of both the historic and contemporary Christian faith experiences are the following: James H. Charlesworth, ed., *Jesus Within Judaism: New Light from Existing Archaeological Discoveries* (New York: Doubleday Books, 1988); Lloyd Gaston, *Paul and the Torah* (Vancouver: University of British Columbia Press, 1987); Pinchas Lapide, *Israelis, Jews, and Jesus*, trans. P. Heinegg (Garden City, N.Y.: Doubleday Books, 1979); John P. Meier, *A Marginal Jew: Rethinking the Historical Jesus* (New York: Doubleday Books, 1991); and Ellis Rivkin, *What Crucified Jesus?* (Nashville, Abingdon Press, 1984).

Notes

1. Fackenheim, Greenberg, Maza, Rubenstein, Cargas, Alice Eckardt, McGarry, Pawlikowski, Roth, Ruether, and others all contributed to my two-volume collection of essays, *Contemporary Jewish Religious Responses to the Shoah* and *Contemporary Christian Religious Responses to the Shoah* (Lanham, Md.: University Press of America, 1993). My own contribution, in the first volume, is entitled "Judaism and Christianity After Auschwitz," pages 1-23.

2. See, also, his important companion volume *Documents of Destruction: Germany and Jewry 1933-1945* (Chicago: Quadrangle Books, 1971).

3. See, also, her critique of contemporary historians and the *Shoah, The Holocaust and the Historians* (Cambridge, Mass.: Harvard University Press, 1981).

4. Chapters 3, 4, and 5, essentially the heart of this book, address as they do the *practical manifestations* of Jewish life after the *Shoah*. They point, again and again, to the *fact* that the reality of the *Shoah* is all but ignored, in the main, by religious Jewish life, responding and reacting as if it never happened. Questions of legal authority for Jewish doing and the rationales for living Jewishly after the *Shoah* are, likewise, *not* addressed in the vol-

umes cited as resources for these chapters, important and significant as they are. Needless to say, and equally as obvious, responding *directly* to the needs and concerns of the Second Generation is virtually nonexistent.

5. Partisan accounts of contemporary events may, also, be found in *The Jerusalem Post*, International Edition and *The Near East Report*, the latter published by The American-Israel Public Affairs Committee (AIPAC).

Glossary

Aliyah: Immigration *to* Israel. Literally, a "going up" to the Land of Israel. (Its opposite is *yeridah*, literally a "going down" from the Land of Israel.)

Ale malei rachamim: "O God, full of compassion." Prayer text included in Jewish funerals, asking Divine blessing and eternal caring upon the deceased.

Antisemitism: Hatred of the Jewish people and the Jewish religious faith, heritage, and tradition. Throughout history, the forms antisemitism have taken have included expulsion, ghettoization, forced religious conversion, denial of civil rights, and extermination-annihilation. (Preferred spelling here is *without* the hyphen; to use a hyphen is to imply its opposite, that there is such a thing as "Semitism," which is nonexistent.)

Aseret ha-Dibrot: Usually translated as the "Ten Commandments," as found in the Torah in *Shemot* (Exodus) 20 and *Devarim* (Deuteronomy) 5. A more accurate translation would be the "Ten Essential Statements," without which no society could endure.

Bar or Bat Mitzvah: Literally, "son" or "daughter of the Commandment." The "coming of age" in the Jewish religious tradition of a boy at age 13 and a girl at age 12 years plus 1 day (girls maturing faster than boys). Usually the ceremony involves the conduct of any or all of a worship service, the reading or chanting selected portions of Scripture, and a speech, possibly a commentary on that Scripture. Usually celebrated with, at times, too elaborate social parties.

Behirah: "Chosenness." The biblical understanding of the children of Israel "chosen" by God for a special purpose, to be "a light unto the nations and a banner unto the peoples," giving evidence by the lives led of a true commitment and following in the ways of God. Over the course of the centuries, this concept has led to misunderstanding between Jews and Christians as well as to false claims of arrogance and superiority on the part of Jews and a desire to supersede them on the part of those who were not.

Ben or Bat Am Yehudi: Literally, "son" or "daughter of the Jewish people." Because of the inherent difficulties affirming the notion of "Commandment" after the *Shoah*, my preferred term for this coming of age experience (open to change, suggestion, modification).

Brith: The "covenant" entered into between God and the children of Israel at Sinai after their escape from Egypt and their wanderings in the Desert, prior to their entrance into the Promised Land of Israel. According to *Devarim* (Deuteronomy), entered into both with those at Sinai as well as with the generations yet to come. *If* Israel honors God and follows in God's ways, *then* God will protect and save Israel from its enemies.

Borei Olam: God as "Creator of the world or universe." The place at which all Jewish theological investigation must begin; the place at which the Torah, the sacred Scriptures of the Jewish people, itself begins. In the aftermath of the *Shoah*, for me, the only initially logical and honest concept still able to address contemporary reality.

Brith Milah: Literally, the "covenant of circumcision." The religious ceremony marking the entre of an 8-day-old Jewish boy into the "covenant of Abraham" by his parents and welcoming him into the Jewish community. The ceremony consists of two distinct parts: the attendant religious ritual and the actual surgical procedure of the removal of the additional flap of skin covering the head of the penis. (Debate continues as to its medical benefits as well as its religious value.)

Cohanim: "Priests." In ancient Israel, the community was divided into three groups: the priests, the Levitical assistants, and the remainder of the community of Israel. The priests were the first to perform the rituals associated with both the portable Ark and the Temple in Jerusalem, assisted by the Levites.

Chuppah: The canopy under which the bride and groom are married. Can be erected in either the congregational sanctuary, the home or the outdoors. Symbolic of the future home (marriage bed?) of the new family.

Chutzpah: "Brazenness." That special quality of stubborn determination associated with the Jewish people that has enabled us to survive despite all previous attempts at our demise.

Die Endlosung: The "'final solution' to the Jewish problem" as understood by Adolf Hitler, may his name be blotted out, and his Nazi minions. Put into practice, it ultimately resulted in the deaths of almost 6 million Jewish men, women, and children; 1 million below the age of 12 and an additional 500,000 between the ages of 12 and 18, in ghettos, concentration camps, and environments in ways that continue to stain the conscience of Western civilization, not only Germany and Poland.

Eretz Yisrael: The "Land of Israel." That place promised by God to the children of Israel according to the Torah and sacred to the religious traditions of Judaism, Christianity, and Islam. Interestingly and significantly enough, the Torah itself posits more than one set of geographic boundaries for the land. The Land of Israel continues to be a source of political and religious dissension in the world today, as yet unresolved.

Get: "Jewish bill of divorcement." Granted by the husband to the wife in Orthodox religious circles and to each other in Conservative religious circles. Historically, Reform Judaism did not make use of this document, accepting, instead, the civil decree of divorce as sufficient. In recent years, however, Reform liturgists and religious thinkers have presented models of such documents, though no "official" one currently exists.

Haftarah: The *additional* scriptural selection associated with the Torah service in the worship service. Usually taken from either prophetic literature or the additional writings found in Scripture, a word, a phrase, a name or an idea contained within it related directly to the primary scriptural selection taken directly from the first Five Books of Moses.

Hagaddah: The special "prayer book" associated with the celebration of *Pesach* (Passover). Literally, "The Story," its essence, surrounded by both prayers and commentaries, involves the retelling of the wondrous and miraculous liberation by God of the Children of Israel from slavery and bondage in Egypt as first recorded in the *Sefer Shemot* (Book of Exodus). (Historically, such an event is *not* recorded in Egyptian documents, however.)

Halakhah: Literally, "the way." The system of Jewish law as culled by the rabbis from the Torah itself and elaborated upon in the Talmud and subsequent and additional Jewish resource literature. For the Orthodox Jew, Jewish law governs all facets and aspects of daily and religious living, coming as it does directly from God and interpreted authoritative by rabbinic spokes*men*. Conservative Judaism likewise affirms its sanctity, but attempts to give it a more human cast through its Law and Standards Committee of its Rabbinical Assembly. Reform Judaism has long rejected its sovereignty, acknowledging, instead, that "the past shall exercise a vote, not a veto" (attributed to the late Rabbi Dr. Solomon Freehof of Rodef Sholom Temple, Pittsburgh).

Hanukkat Ha-Bayit: The ceremony that marks the "dedication of the [new] home" by the affixing of the *mezzuzah* and other attendant rituals (see later).

Har Sinai: "Mount Sinai" in the Negev Desert. The sight at which, supposedly, God entered into covenant with the children of Israel after first liberating them from Egyptian slavery.

Holocaust: Up until recently, the universally acknowledged English word used to describe the wanton murder of nearly 6 million Jews by the Nazis and their collaborators. Said to have first been used by the noted writer and Nobel Prize winner Elie Wiesel. Its origin is the Anglicization of the Greek translation of the Hebrew word *'olah*, the totally consumable offering by fire to God as depicted in the Torah. In recent years, the term itself has become increasingly problematic for obvious reasons. Current thinking is to use the Hebrew word *Shoah* instead (see later).

Kaddish: Aramaicized prayer usually understood to be the "mourner's prayer" recited by the survivors after the funeral of a loved one either during the worship service or at home. Reform Judaism, on the other hand, has suggested that, after the *Shoah*, *all* Jews are mourners and has the entire congregation stand and recite this prayer.

Ketubah: "Jewish marriage contract" given by the husband to the wife and spelling out the terms and conditions of the marital agreement in both Orthodox and Conservative religious communities. Reform Judaism initially rejected its use as unequal and condescending, but, in recent years, has sought to revive it with a more egalitarian text.

Kiddushin: "Holiness" or "sanctification." The term used to describe Jewish marriage. There is literally no linguistic equivalency in Hebrew for our English word *marriage*.

Korban: The "sacrificial animal" in the ancient cultic system of worship in biblical times, both pre-Temple and Temple; still associated today with the *Pesach* (Passover) liturgy as the *korban Pesach*, the Passover sacrifice, reminiscent of that system.

Leviim: The "Levitical priests" whose primary function was to assist the *Cohanim*, priests, in the performance of their pre-Temple and Temple cultic rituals and to be responsible for and care for the *clai kodesh*, the "holy vessels" associated with these rituals.

Machzor: The special "prayer book" of the Jewish religious tradition used for the High Holy Days of *Rosh ha-Shanah* (New Year) and *Yom Kippur* (Day of Atonement) only.

Madrega: A term from medieval philosophic Hebrew used to describe a plane or state of spiritual existence and awareness.

Megillah: Generically any "scroll," *Megillah* or *Megillat Esther* is that associated with the festival of *Purim* (Lots) and tells the story found in the Book of Esther in the Torah.

Menorah: Generally, an candelabrum, the most well-known the eight-branched one associated with the festival of *Hanukkah* (Dedication). A seven-branched one is reminiscent of that found in the ancient Temple in Jerusalem, echoing the first story in *Bereshit* (Genesis), that of creation and the seven days of the week.

Mercaz ruchani: "Spiritual center." A term attributed to Ahad Ha-Am (Asher Ginzburg, 1856-1927), one of the early Zionist intellectual giants of pre-State Israel, whose vision for the state was that of a place where the cultural and religious essences of Judaism and the Jewish people would continue to flower and develop, spreading to all parts of the world where Jews dwell and enriching the lives of non-Jews as well.

Mezzuzah: The cylindrical container housing two sections of Torah: *Devarim* (Deuteronomy) 6:4-9 and 11:13-21, in response to the biblical injunction, also in *Devarim*, "You shall write them upon the doorposts of thy house and upon thy gates, that ye may remember and do all My commandments and be holy unto your God."

Midrash: Jewish interpretive literature of a nonlegal nature. Commentary on the Torah as well as additional sermonic and story literature "filling in the gaps," so to speak, in the literary record. Some of it is quite fanciful, allowing the Rabbis, the creators of *midrashic* literature, to give free rein to their imaginations. Others of it are quite insightful, morally, ethically, spiritually, psychologically, as well as intellectually.

Mitzvot: Literally, "commanded act" by God to the Jewish people. The continuum referred to in this book, and terribly problematic after the *Shoah*, is that of *Mitzaveh-mitzvot-mitzuvim*, Commander-commandments-commanded. According to the Rabbis, 613 "commandments" are found throughout the Torah of both a moral-ethical and ritual-ceremonial nature, of equal sanctity. The commandments of a Torah given by God ultimately become in the eyes of the Rabbis the legal system, *Halakhah*, of the Jewish religious tradition. The word has also taken on a popular form in describing any "good deed."

Mohel: Jewish "Ritual circumcisor," usually a rabbi or cantor, well-versed in both the ritual traditions and the surgical procedures.

Pharisees: The radical and revolutionary class of Jews who, after the destruction of the Second Temple in the year 70 C.E. by the Romans, saved both Judaism and the Jewish people by reinterpreting the "system of Judaism," calling for study of sacred texts, divine worship, and high ethical behavior. Contemporary religious expressions of Judaism are the descendants of their innovations. Misunderstood by the New Testament writers, specially those who wrote the Gospels, in all likelihood, they would have had more in common with Jesus than their competitors, the Sadducees, who wished to affirm the status quo and return to the priestly system.

Pidyon ha-Ben: The symbolic birth ceremony of "redeeming" the 1-month-old Israelite boy from priestly service. Still practiced by both Orthodox and Conservative Jews, it was abandoned by Reform Jews as not representative of the equality of males and females.

Second Generation: The term now used to describe we children of *Shoah* survivors, children of severely diminished families, who are now adults ourselves. Many of us continue to struggle with the *Shoah*, some psychologically and others religiously.

Sh'losh regalim: The three "pilgrimage festivals" according to the Torah when the ancient Israelites would journey to Jerusalem and present their gift offerings at the Temple: *Pesach* (Passover), *Shavuot* (Festival of Weeks), and *Sukkot* (Festival of Booths).

Shoah: The Hebrew, biblical term now preferred more and more to describe the wanton murder and callous slaughter of almost 6 million Jewish men, women, and children during the years 1939-1945 by the Nazis and their assistants. Best translated as "Destruction" or "Devastation." A singularly unique event in the history of the Jewish people as well as all humankind.

Shofar: "Ram's horn," a reminder of the *Bereshit* (Genesis) story wherein Abraham sacrificed a ram rather than his son Isaac. Used in ancient Israel as both a military instrument and a call to gather the community. Associated today with the High Holy Days of *Rosh ha-Shanah* (New Year) and *Yom Kippur* (Day of Atonement).

Siddur: The special Jewish "prayer book" for use at *Shabbat* (Sabbath) and *Haggim* (festival) services, as distinct from the *Machzor* used for the High Holy Days only.

Torah sheb'al peh: Literally, "Torah that is upon the mouth." The Oral Tradition of Rabbinic interpretation later set down in such primary texts as the *Mishnah* and *Talmud*. The so-called oral tradition continues to remain authoritative today for Orthodox Jews, less so for Conservative, Reform, and Reconstructionist Jews.

Torah shebichtav: Literally, "Torah that is written down." The written text that begins with *Bereshit* (Genesis) and ends with *Divrei Hayamim Bet* (Second Chronicles).

Vidui: The "confessional prayer" text to be said by the religious Jew prior to death asking God's forgiveness for any sins committed and not yet atoned. There are such prayers in all Jewish denominations.

V'shamru: Popular *Shabbat* (Sabbath) hymn emphasizing both the covenant and the creation story.

Yahrtzeit: Literally, "year time." The term acknowledging the anniversary of the death of a loved one. On such anniversaries, the names of the deceased are called out at the conclusion of the worship service and *Kaddish* is said by the mourners.

Yeridah: Emigration *from* Israel. Literally, a "going down" from the Land of Israel. (See its opposite, *aliyah*, a "going up" to the Land of Israel.)

Yesurin shel ahavah: Literally, "chastisements out of love." The rabbinic tradition of examining critically those aspects of Jews life out of a sense of deep commitment and caring. The objective of such critical analysis is to improve, never to destroy, governed as it must be by love of one's fellow Jews and one's Jewish tradition, however interpreted.

Yism'chu: Popular *Shabbat* (Sabbath) hymn emphasizing creation rather than creation and covenant.

Zeman matan Torahteinu: Literally, "the time of the giving of the Torah." The summary description of the festival of *Simchat Torah* (Joy of the Torah) coming at the end of the festival of *Sukkot* (Booths).

THE BOOKS OF THE TORAH

The Five Books of Moses

Bereshit	Genesis
Shemot	Exodus
Vayikra	Leviticus
Bamidbar	Numbers
Devarim	Deuteronomy

Nevi'im: The Prophets

Yehoshua	Joshua
Shoftim	Judges
Shmuel Alef	I Samuel
Shmuel Bet	II Samuel
Melachim Alef	I Kings
Melachim Bet	II Kings
Yishayahu	Isaiah
Yirmiyahu	Jeremiah
Yehezkel	Ezekiel

The Twelve

Hoshai'ah	Hosea
Yoel	Joel
Amos	Amos

Ovadyah	Obadiah
Yonah	Jonah
Micha	Micah
Nachum	Nahum
Havakkuk	Habakkuk
Tzfanyah	Zephaniah
Haggai	Haggai
Zecharyah	Zechariah
Malachi	Malachi

Ketuvim: The Writings

Tehillim	Psalms
Mishlei	Proverbs
Iyov	Job
Shir ha-Shirim	Song of Songs; Canticles
Rut	Ruth
Aicah	Lamentations
Kohelet	Ecclesiastes
Esther	Esther
Daniel	Daniel
Ezra	Ezra
Nehemyah	Nehemiah
Divrei ha-Yamim Alef	I Chronicles
Divrei ha-Yamim Bet	II Chronicles

THE JEWISH HOLIDAYS

Biblical—Major

Shabbat	Sabbath
Pesach	Passover
Sefirat ha-Omer	Counting of the Omer
Shavuot	Weeks
Rosh ha-Shanah	New Year
Yom Kippur	Day of Atonement
Sukkot	Booths
Shemini Atzeret	Eighth Day of Solemn Assembly
Rosh Hodesh	New Moon

Biblical—Minor

Hanukkah	Festival of Dedication
Purim	Festival of Esther or Lots

Rabbinic

Lag b'Omer	33rd Day of the Omer
Tisha b'Av	9th Day of Av, Collective Day of Mourning
Simchat Torah	Celebration of the Torah
Tu b'Shevat	15th Day of Shevat, Jewish Arbor Day

Contemporary

Yom ha-Shoah	*Shoah* Remembrance Day
Yom ha-Atzmaut	Israeli Independence Day

THE MONTHS OF THE JEWISH CALENDAR

Tishri	September-October
Heshvan	October-November
Kislev	November-December
Tevet	December-January
Shevat	January-February
Adar (also	
Adar Bet or II)	February-March
Nisan	March-April
Iyar	April-May
Sivan	May-June
Tammuz	June-July
Av	July-August
Elul	August-September

About the Author

Steven L. Jacobs serves as the rabbi of Temple B'nai Sholom, Huntsville, Alabama, and teaches Jewish Studies at Oakwood College, Huntsville, and Mississippi State University, Starkville. He received his B.A. (with distinction) from the Pennsylvania State University, University Park, and his B.H.L., M.A.H.L., D.H.L., and rabbinic ordination from the Hebrew Union College-Jewish Institute of Religion, Cincinnati, Ohio. In addition to serving congregations in Steubenville, Ohio, Niagara Falls, New York, Birmingham and Mobile, Alabama, and Dallas, Texas, he has taught at Spring Hill College, Mobile, Alabama, University of Alabama, Tuscaloosa, University of Alabama at Birmingham, Birmingham-Southern College, and Samford University, Birmingham. Author of more than fifty scholarly articles and reviews dealing primarily with the *Shoah*, his books include *Shirot Bialik: A New and Annotated Translation of Chaim Nachman Bialik's Epic Poems* (Columbus: Alpha Publishing Company, 1987), *Raphael Lemkin's Thoughts on Nazi Genocide: Not Guilty?* (Lewiston, N.Y.: The Edwin Mellen Company, 1992), *Contemporary Jewish Religious Responses to the Shoah* and *Contemporary Christian Religious Responses to the Shoah* (Lanham, Md.: University Press of America, 1993). He serves on the Alabama State Holocaust Advisory Council and as an Educational Consultant to the Center on the Holocaust, Genocide and Human Rights, Philadelphia. He is, also, the editor of the papers of the late Raphael Lemkin, the "father" of the United Nations Treaty on Genocide. He is married to the former Louanne Clayton; they have three children: Hannah, Naomi, and Shea.

Note

Because Steven Jacobs believes so strongly in the concept of "Covenants of Dialogue," you are to feel free to write him in response to this book at Post Office Box 2463, Huntsville, Alabama 35804-2463.